# PRAISE FOR ARTEMES

If you're seeking a radical and comprehensive new approach to the huge challenges we face as humanity, rooted in ancient wisdom with modern insights, make sure you check out Artemes.

*Shamash Alidina, Author of Mindfulness for Dummies*

I approached this book with more than a little skepticism. However, I found Artemes to be a refreshingly honest critique of modern capitalism and it has left me more hopeful, not less.

With extraordinary dexterity, Beverly takes the reader on an educated tour of the trends that are redefining the way we work and do business, and provides the tools and methodologies needed to help kick-start these changes.

*Cody Saxton, Prominent Book Reviewer*

Humanity is on the brink of evolution. What we need for that to take place are individuals down on the ground who are challenging the current paradigm, and creating new ways that dismantle the old. In this book, Joel Beverly not only presents a system for social change, but also a pathway forward for creating more peace, love, equality, and consciousness in our world. Highly recommended for anyone who wants to see change in our world, and is ready to be part of a new revolution on reality.

*Tracey Ash, Ascension Global Leader and Author of Reality Revolution*

Through all my years in blockchain and cryptocurrency I have never seen anything like this. This is cryptocurrency with a heart and soul. Artemes could be priceless for humanity.

*Preston Smith, Founder, Nexus Platform*

## Some of the 200+ verified Amazon reviews:

Joel brings first hand knowledge and solutions for economic disparity. In a world of much divisiveness, it's refreshing to dive into a common approach for solutions.

*Rick Seals*

This book is a breath of fresh air. It is well written and is just what our society needs to move from a culture of rage to one of compassion and reason.

*Mike Cummings*

Beverly has put forth a concept, tools, and training that could provide a foundation for systemic change in how the world operates.

*Meg Thornton*

Anyone who is interested in learning more about how to deal with the challenges facing the world, whether locally or globally, should check this book out. The realities of COVID-19, social unrest, and national division make this book even more relevant.

*Joseph Fluder*

I honestly picked this up with a lot of skepticism after a friend recommended it. But I was genuinely blown away by this guy's vision for a very different kind of system for our world, and I'm kinda hooked on the idea that now might actually be the moment when something like this could work.

*Sylvie Di*

# ARTEMES

A Conscious Economic System
for Creating Equality in an
Unbalanced World

**By Joel Beverly**

# ARTEMES

A Conscious
Economic
System for
Creating
Equality in an
Unbalanced
World

JOEL **BEVERLY**

## Artemes Publishing
## 2020 United States

Copyright 2020, Artemes.

## Visit Artemes.global for more details.

The opinions expressed in this book are those of the author. This book contains advice and information relating to creating a message for social change. All efforts have been made to ensure the accuracy of the information contained in this book as of the date of publication. The reader takes full responsibility for their use of this information. The publisher and the author disclaim liability for any outcomes that may occur as a result of applying the methods suggested in this book.

Front Cover Design Aleksandar Milosavljevic
Edited by Lois Rose
ISBN 978-1-7356838-0-5
Library of Congress number:2020916913
Book design by smhdesign.ir

Dedicated to all the individuals who are striving to make this world a fairer and more equal place.

# Table of Contents

# INTRODUCTION

The world, as we know it, is undergoing a period of accelerated change. Many of the old structures that no longer serve us—either personally or socially—are on the verge of breaking down, and as of yet, we have not found consistent and meaningful ways to replace them.

Even the strongest among us have felt powerless in these times: a nagging feeling that there is something we should be doing to address the issues that impact our world, and a sense that we don't know what the solutions could be. Maybe you are among those who are looking at the environmental issues, the socio-political climate, the gaps in the economy, and wondering what you can do to make a difference in our world today. Perhaps you've wanted to stand up and come forward, to do something effective, to break the cycles that plague humanity, yet without the guidance of clear leadership or innovative and accessible solutions, you may have found yourself remaining inactive, and unable to make a contribution that impacts meaningful change.

If you've been feeling that calling—the sense that you are supposed to contribute in some way but that you just don't know how—you are definitely not alone. There has never been such a period in history where the future of our planet seemed so uncertain, where the social structures have felt so disparate and divided, where the systems feel like they have been created so that only a handful can win. Yet in this pivotal time, where there is so much uncertainty and fear, there is also a profound opportunity for mass change to occur.

If you are feeling the calling to be part of that change, in the pages that follow, I will be offering you a solution-focused model that provides you with an incentive to be part of a wave that impacts humanity at its core. You'll be invited to be part of a movement which offers practical solutions that can be applied to address some of the key issues that impact humanity as a whole. That system is known as Artemes, and it's one that you can become involved with immediately, starting today.

## Introducing the Artemes System

There are three major challenges with the way that our current system is functioning as a whole.

## 1 - ECONOMY

Our economy thrives on creating "winners and losers." The number of people who are able to win at this game is diminishing rapidly in these times, as the economic gaps continue to grow wider, throwing many of us into a state of survival where only the elite can thrive.

## 2 - LEADERSHIP

The leaders of the systems that govern us—those who have risen to power—lack the incentive or motivation to disrupt a system that fundamentally benefits them.

## 3 - UNCONSCIOUSNESS

Most of humanity is not awake to the true reality of this moment. We are asleep at the wheel, distracted by social media, TV, alcohol, drugs, shopping, food, sex, porn, and so on. These addictions inhibit us from creating a more meaningful world for ourselves.

And so the cycle worsens.

At this stage, we have two options. To try and fix the current paradigm, which is already clearly broken, or to offer an opposing system that addresses these issues. Artemes is this opposing system. For the first time in history, we are offered a model that addresses all of these issues simultaneously.

1. To address the issue of socio-economic disparity, Artemes offers a conscious cryptocurrency system designed to create a fairer distribution of wealth.

2. To counteract the imbalance in leadership, Artemes has a "Council of the Aware"—eleven world leaders who direct a share of the cryptocurrency wealth generation to address global issues.

3. To overcome our tendency to check out, Artemes offers a path for the conscious revolution of self, which supports

both those involved in the system to evolve personally, and humanity's evolution as a whole.

These three elements combined create Artemes: a system that challenges our current paradigm on all levels.

## (1) The Artemes Cryptocurrency System

The cryptocurrency system is the economic driver for Artemes and what we might call 'altruistic capitalism.' It's a blockchain-based system of wealth sharing which is built upon equality. In recent years, we've seen great shifts in the way that economics can function, with the advent of Bitcoin and other crypto-based currencies. So far, most of these new economies have been similar to the old systems—benefiting the few rather than the whole. Now imagine one that was not focused on personal gain, but was put to use for the benefit of all. In contrast to other economic systems that are designed to increase gaps, Artemes is designed to close them. It's a system that supports both the one and the many at the same time.

## [2] Aware Leadership

This system differs from our current paradigm because it steers the cryptocurrency wealth share away from a focus on personal gain towards one on the good of all. A Council of the Aware: eleven leaders—known and trusted globally because they are at the pinnacle of their spiritual growth—will control a portion of the Artemes blockchain and will guide the ship with respect to where and how this wealth is distributed. Each leader will choose eleven trusted and awakened advisors (each covering a distinct specialty) that will help them manage and lead. Each of these trusted advisors will then choose a further eleven awakened individuals, and these eleven will select eleven more. And suddenly this cryptocurrency system isn't just another way to create personal wealth. Now it has a heart and a soul, and a mechanism enabling it to spread across the world. How much more likely are we willing to invest and partake in a system when we know that the profits are going to the very causes that we hold dear?

### [3] - Artemes Training

The Artemes Training is designed to further your own awakening. This nondenominational, heart-centered training enables you to experience more awareness and break out of any pre-programmed reality that you may be unconsciously operating in. I'll be presenting much of this training in the pages that follow.

Wealth and power have often been used to create negative and undesirable impacts in the world that we are living in today. Some of the biggest challenges our society faces are rooted in the fact that wealth and power have been used as destructive forces for personal gain. With the Artemes System, we flip the script on this, putting the wealth to work for good, restructuring the relationship between wealth and power at its very core. In addition, when you begin to engage in Artemes—whether through the cryptocurrency economy or practicing the teachings presented in this book—the inter-relational nature of Artemes means that every contribution you make affects the whole. And you don't have to wait to start making an impact. Artemes is structured in a way that enables you to begin making a powerful impact with the actions that you take, and that impact starts today.

**ARTEMES**
A Conscious Economic System for Creating
Equality in an Unbalanced World

# PART ONE 1

# WHERE WE ARE NOW

# CHAPTER ONE

## ARTEMES: OUR VISION FOR A NEW WORLD

At this point in time, it is crucial that each and every one of us awakens, and fortunately for us all, we are perfectly positioned for this revolution to unfold.

It seems that humanity, as we know it, is on the verge of a breakdown. Many of us have felt this deeply both on a personal level, and on a societal level. Individually, each one of us has likely experienced a feeling of being close to breaking. This may have been a fleeting sense that comes and goes, or it may have been all-pervading—a feeling that takes over and never seems to leave. On a societal level, the constant barrage of news and information that we receive on a daily basis— from environmental destruction, to mass shootings, to hate crimes, to the mistreatment of immigrants, to incidents of war or terror, to the global refugee crisis—has left many of us in despair, feeling hopeless for the future of humanity, and with the question of whether it is too late to make any meaningful impact at all.

Yet, despite the collective challenges we face, this mass breakdown offers us a rare opportunity for the awakening of mass consciousness. Regardless of our resistance to it, and our fear of the outcome, being close to breaking can actually be a good thing. As the ancient Persian poet Rumi once said, "The wound is the place where the light enters you," and we all have the exact wound that we need right now for this mass awakening to occur.

What we need for that to happen is a more acceptable kind of spiritual path for the twenty-first century being. An accessible, decentralized way forward that is simple and trustworthy to all. This path does not take the place of any preferred religion, but complements it instead. It's a spiritual path to awakening that creates an even deeper space for whatever views we might currently hold.

We need a path that creates a chain reaction in the world that we currently live in, so that one person, then ten, then ten thousand, then a billion awaken, until eventually we have one awakened humanity. A tidal wave of awareness. A conscious revolution for all. As a species, this is our potential, and the next step on our evolutionary journey.

## WHERE IT ALL WENT WRONG

Before we consider our path to this awakening, it's essential to highlight what we are actually awakening from. Although it is not possible to pinpoint an exact moment where the spiraling issues that we currently face began to intensify, a look at our recent history reveals a common theme. In the US, and in other countries of the Western world, the '60s and '70s were periods where we collectively had a stronger sense of community and social connection. But the direction of our path began to change in the '80s, where we developed a greater focus on individual success, and on "I, me, and mine." Since then, we have become so focused on the journey of the self, the "winner takes all" mentality, and the sense that we are entitled to continue gaining at the expense of those around us, that many of us have disconnected from our social responsibility and our sense of creating a fairer world for all. As a result, the economic gaps are widening, and the gaps between those who own the most and those who own the least are increasing by the day. (We'll explore the statistics behind just how much these gaps are growing in the chapters that follow.)

In our major cities, we see mass homelessness, a situation that comedian Aziz Ansari commented on in his 2019 Netflix show *Right Now* by saying:

> *Don't you realize in fifty years we're all going to look back and feel like complete assholes? Like, isn't that the dream, in a way, that fifty years from now we look back and we can't even justify ourselves to our grandkids. We're just sitting there like, "I don't know what the fuck was going on, there were just homeless people everywhere and no-one gave a shit. Er . . . just kind of avoid eye contact, walk around them, hope it wasn't one of the ones that chased you down: every now and then they'd have cups out and you'd open up your wallet and be like, 'Oh sorry, all I got is twenties," and then you'd hop on one of those weird scooters and get the fuck out of there. It was a weird time, 2019.[1]*

A similar view was offered by 2020 presidential candidate Marianne Williamson in an interview with comedian and activist, Russell Brand. She shared to a largely spiritual audience, "You can't not cultivate justice, not cultivate mercy, not cultivate democracy, not cultivate compassion, not look at mass incarceration because it's not in your neighborhood, not look at wealth inequality because it's not in your neighborhood, not look at what is happening to the food supply because you can drink green juice. You can't do that and then be all shocked when this explosion of disfunction and anti-democratic assault happens."[2]

Over 41 million US residents are food insecure. This is over 12 percent of the country's population. In New York, in one of the wealthiest cities in the US, we learn that over 1 million people are food insecure.[3] This means that in a city of 8 million, one-eighth of the population, including children and the elderly, don't know where their next meal is coming from. The homelessness and food insecurity issue is not just reserved for the larger cities of the world either. Here in East Kentucky, where I live, the poverty rate is over 29 percent, meaning that nearly a third of the people live below the poverty line.[4] A friend and former mayor estimates that in my hometown of Hazard, among a population of 5,000, more than twenty-five people are homeless. I see them using the bridges and the downtown parking garage as shelter. In nearby Isom, a pantry that is restocked nightly with food is emptied each night by the homeless and food insecure with these individuals taking refuge at a vacant coal tipple.

As hedge fund billionaire Ray Dalio famously said, "The trickle-down process of having money at the top trickle down to workers

and others by improving their earnings and creditworthiness is not working—the system of making capitalism work well for most people is broken."[5]

In *The Killing Fields of Inequality*, Swedish global social scientist Göran Therborn highlights, "Inequality always means excluding some people from something. When it doesn't literally kill people or stunt their lives, inequality means exclusion: excluding people from possibilities produced by human development."[6] So we not only need to concern ourselves with homelessness, but also the fact that certain groups are being excluded from opportunities that enable them to progress fairly.

These examples do not suggest that we are broken and we need to be fixed. It's just that we have the potential for so much more. What we need to heal this social and spiritual epidemic that touches so many of us is a system that enables us to wake up, *tune back into our compassion for humanity*, remember our social values, and take action from our heart.

## HOW THE CHANGE BEGINS

It is true that many of the changes that need to occur are showing up on multiple levels in the world around us. When we think of tackling the multitude of issues that we collectively face, many of us have been frequently left with a feeling that there is nothing we can do. Yet the seeds of the conscious revolution are much more accessible than you may realize. They don't actually start outside of ourselves. Instead, they start in your mind, with you.

In order for the current paradigm to change, although much must alter on the outside, it is our inner climate—our perceptions, and our ability to operate from a state of aware consciousness and make meaningful changes—that needs the most immediate attention. We are being called to individually and spiritually awaken in these times, so that we act from a place of consciousness, rather than reacting from a place of fear.

When you deeply challenge the way you see and perceive the world, it begins to impact your actions. What starts in your mind as a conscious choice to change your thinking, dismantle your programming, deconstruct your perceptions, challenge your fears, and create more awareness, filters into the way you behave in the world around you. For the issues that seemed unyielding, once you no longer view them through the lens of fear and hopelessness, you suddenly see a promising path forward. What once seemed like the destruction of humanity is viewed as a powerful new beginning for us all. And so we build a network of individuals globally who are not just awakening for their own benefit—they are awakening so they can make a meaningful contribution to humanity. And one by one, that network grows, until we reach a tipping point: millions worldwide taking responsibility for their own awakening so that they can contribute to something more.

As I write this book, I have a dear friend who is totally desolate. She told me that one night as she lay in bed trying to sleep, she noticed that her teeth were permanently clenched. She said she felt like she was living in a virtual hell. She has all this stress because she doesn't have healthcare. She constantly worries that at any moment she, or her husband, will get sick and lose everything they have worked their

entire lives for. Maybe you have similar fears or can relate to that feeling.

We need to deeply question the structure of a society that creates a situation where the humans within it are forced to live in such fear. How, as a society, have we normalized allowing our friends and neighbors to be tortured in this way? Although these questions have become political and, as I write this, are currently taking a front seat at the Democratic presidential debates for the 2020 candidate, this is actually much more of a humanitarian than a political question. Whatever our political affiliation, if we are not for taking care of our fellow humans, we have gotten too lost in our heads to know right from wrong. It is time for us to come together and understand that we are only as great as our most vulnerable individual.

The fear that many experience from the possibility of going broke because of a health issue is not a Republican or Democratic issue. It's tied more to the issue of how a lack of financial resources triggers us into fear. I was born into—and live in—a part of the world that is economically deprived, and I've seen clearly how we are grossly conditioned into accepting the socio-economic divisions that we are born into. When I talk to those around me about everyone in the world being taken care of—whether with healthcare, education, or money to support a fair lifestyle—I am often met with the reply, "Everyone should work hard for what they get. There's no such thing as a free lunch."

Yet many are born into a world where they do not have to work for what they have. They shuffle an inheritance from here to there and become a Trump, an Al Gore, or a Kardashian, often without having to truly work for anything. Yet those around me weren't given the tools to question the very system that disenfranchises them and makes the game unfair for them.

From the perspective of the current game we are playing, one child can be born with more opportunities and prospects than another—like starting a basketball game with one team 20 points ahead—and we call this system fair. We have to change the rules in order to make it fairer. I quote again from *The Killing Fields of Inequality,* "The rights of all children to a good enabling childhood should be a principle political guideline."[7]

In the current system, the winners of the game are also the ones who make the rules, so the system keeps perpetuating. What are the chances of the rules ever being changed to really help those who are at a disadvantage from the perspective of the system, when the rule-makers themselves are the ones that benefit? If you ever studied Game Theory, you will know that it's not likely.

The first step in fixing this game is to end the created division between winners and losers and to level the playing field so that we all start with the same advantages. The point of Artemes is to create a fun, new game.

Besides creating a new economic structure that is fairer to all, Artemes offers a way to shift our perspective so that we want to play the game more fairly. Built into the Artemes System that is presented in this book is an invitation to awaken, and to take responsibility for our own level of consciousness as part of our world awakening. When we are awake, our

compassion is activated and we care about each other, so that the game starts to change. This is also reflected in the wider Artemes System in that it is directed by the Council of the Aware (you'll learn more about them in chapter 4). Their awareness determines the way the money invested in Artemes is put to good causes and healing in our world.

Later on in this book, we're going to break down the details on how the cryptocurrency economy of the Artemes System offers practical solutions to some of the challenges we face today. But before we get there, we are going to start with you. For the remainder of this chapter, we'll start to look at your conditioning, your programming, your thoughts and your fears. In the chapter that follows, we'll look at increasing your awareness as a path to conscious awakening, and how this impacts your service to humanity. Then, if you resonate with these teachings, and if you want to go deeper, once you've learned more about the conscious cryptocurrency economy and the Council of the Aware that leads it, I'll share a number of simple practices that you can apply in your everyday life so that you can continue to awaken.

## The Paralysis of Fear

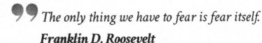 *The only thing we have to fear is fear itself.*
**Franklin D. Roosevelt**

Fear is one of the forces that holds together this limited world that we know. If we want to escape our current paradigm, we must begin by facing our fears in order to set ourselves free. Yet most of us would rather avoid our fears entirely, and if you think about our reality, it's no surprise that we have learned to sidestep our fear. Everything in our limiting world—from the emotionally numbing medication that is so readily available, to the fast foods that are served on a 24/7 basis, to the porn that is at our fingertips, to the social media feeds that we lose ourselves in, to our smartphones that are the sleeping pills of the masses— *everything* is arranged so that we don't have to feel the truth of what is going on, either inside us or around us. If you've been checked out rather than tuned in, it's because you live in a world where at every corner, you can make a purchase that distracts you from your emotions. We may have made great advances in technology, but one of the greatest prices we human beings have paid for that is that it creates an environment where we are able to be more checked out than we have ever been.

Fear must no longer control our existence. From terror, to hunger, to anger, to hopelessness, to rage, the fear that dominates us must be tackled differently if we are to survive. Overcoming fear is one of our most essential growth edges as a species, and it is doubtful that we will continue if we keep operating with fear at the helm.

The path to eliminating fear starts with the understanding that our thoughts and our worries are not real things, but we allow them to control us to the point of distress. Panic is a state of being in your head. In that space you are paralyzed. You don't take that first step to make things better. Reality seldom affects us as much as the illusory thoughts that torture us. Sometimes our thoughts are dirty, other times they are mean, on occasion they are angry, and often they are sad. These are memories of the past that rear up and strike at us; they are worries of the future that weigh heavily on our being. These daytime dreams can often seem nightmarish. I say 'seem' because they only appear to be real. In reality, they are only thoughts—synapses firing in our head.

Why do we let these "unreal" things affect us so greatly? Why do we spend so much time in this torturous mental arena? And how does this dominance of fear affect our outside world?

Many of us have been thrown into a state of survival in these times, and although the issues that we face are very real, survival is much more of a mental and emotional state than it is an economic one. I say this, not as someone who lives in a bubble and is detached from reality, but rather as someone who grew up and lives in Eastern Kentucky: the second poorest congressional district in the US. As a child growing up, it was almost as if I was raised in a Third World country, hidden deep inside the confines of a First World society. To get water, I dropped a bucket into a hand-dug well and pulled it out one arm's length at a time. I carried it in an old 5-gallon lard bucket, about 200 feet back to the house where it was used for drinking, cooking, bathing, and washing clothes. I shit in an outhouse in the dead of winter. I was hungry at times. Yet I've had the experience of rewriting the survival mindset that this kind of upbringing created, firsthand. What I came to understand is that *survival is a mindset* and it is way more biological than most of us realize. Once we believe that our sense of safety is under threat, or our lives are on the line, our 'reptilian brain' kicks in. It's the ancient part of our brain that was wired to keep us alive. Something crucial about this part of the brain that you need to understand to wake up is: once it kicks in, our higher centers—including our connection to peace, love, compassion, and all the qualities that make us operate as decent human beings—shut down to enable us to survive. *Part of our journey to becoming conscious is developing the ability to interrupt the thought patterns that have hijacked us into fear,* and we need to understand our thought patterns to move beyond any issues we are facing.

We have to calm the waters of our minds so that we can see other options to move forward. Once you see those other options, then you take that first step forward. At first, it is an effort, but with practice, it starts to happen naturally. Towards the end of this book, you'll learn tools that enable you to dismantle your fear as soon as it arises and practices that rewire you so that you are no longer programmed to operate from a place of fear.

If you think it's not possible to operate without fear in these turbulent times, then look to Viktor Frankl for inspiration. Written from a concentration camp in the Second World War, he shares in *Man's Search for Meaning*, "Everything can be taken from a man but one thing: the last of the human freedoms—to choose one's attitude in any given set of circumstances, to choose one's own way."[8]

It is this choice that we will be building upon as we progress through the Artemes System.

## Conditioning

When we start to unpack fear, we realize that it is a conditioned state. Although we are all biologically equipped to feel fear, it is our environment and what we have learned from it that activate this, and other similar states. Individually, we have all been conditioned and molded by society to be exactly what we are. There is no way that we could be anything else at this point in time. Society molds us quickly, and even if we can break free from this, the options that are offered to us hardly ever fit.

At birth, society (our parents, our teachers, our pastors, our governments, our TVs) begins to mold us, and by the time we are seven or eight years old, we are held hostage by the beliefs of who we are. The economically disadvantaged are tortured by thoughts of riches, while the rich are tormented by thoughts of becoming poor. These beliefs and thoughts are what keep each of us locked in our own personal hell. They keep us from quitting our dead-end job, from writing that amazing paper, from painting that masterpiece, from asking for that raise, from making that one phone call, from standing up for ourselves, from creating that life that we dream of.

How can we break free of the societal fabric that locks us into place? To address this challenge, we must go within. This means dismantling the construct of our individual realities, including the misperceptions, programming, beliefs, and the lies that we've all been told that we mistook for truth. Only then can we make the most effective impact for ourselves. Once this is accomplished, we can each creatively foster a new world of potential for ourselves and the world that we exist in.

A conscious revolution is the best hope to move beyond our current paradigm as an individual and as a species. A prerequisite for this revolution is present moment awareness (for obtaining awareness is the most revolutionary thing that each of us can do). We must work to bring this awareness to every individual in every moment. This is the vital work that each and every one of us must undertake so that we are able to come into—and remain in—the moment, and solve our challenges from that place.

## SUMMING UP

In this chapter we've touched upon the collective challenges we face and how solving them begins with tackling our own thought processes, conditioning, and fear.

### We looked at:

- How, in these times, it seems that humanity, as we know it, is on the verge of breaking down.

- Despite the collective challenges we face, this mass breakdown offers us a rare opportunity to awaken mass consciousness.

- We need a more acceptable kind of spiritual path for the twenty-first century being.

- Many of us are lost in a "winner takes all" mentality, and the sense that we are entitled to continue gaining at the expense of those around us.

- The gaps between those who own the most and those who own the least are increasing by the day. For example, over 12 percent of the US population is food insecure.

- What we need to heal this social and spiritual epidemic is to *tune back into our compassion for humanity*, remember our social values, and take action from our heart.

- We are being called to individually and spiritually awaken in these times, so that we act from a place of consciousness, rather than reacting from a place of fear.

- Fear is one of the forces that holds together this limited world that we know. If we want to escape our current paradigm, we must begin by facing our fears.

- The path to eliminating fear starts with the understanding that our thoughts and our worries are not real things.

- Many of us have been thrown into a state of survival in these current times, and although the issues that we face are very real, survival is much more of a mental and emotional state than it is an economic one.

- We have to calm the waters of our minds so that we can see other options to move forward.

- When we start to unpack fear, we realize that it is a conditioned state. Although we are all biologically equipped to feel fear, it is our environment and what we have learned from it that activate this, and other similar states.

Built into the Artemes System that is presented in this book is an invitation to awaken, and to take responsibility for our own consciousness as part of our world awakening as a whole. In the chapter that follows we are going to dive deeper, so that we look at how we can create a crack in our conditioning—so that we can experience higher consciousness, and begin to awaken.

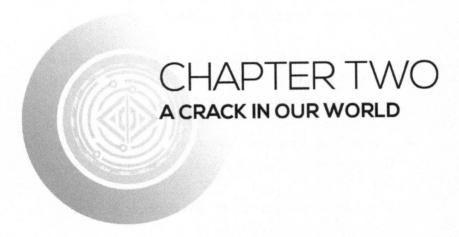

# CHAPTER TWO
## A CRACK IN OUR WORLD

Although many of the issues that we are collectively experiencing need to be tackled externally, one of the biggest challenges that humanity faces exists within each and every one of us.

We may have created a physical world beyond the wildest imaginings of our ancestors—the technological advances we have made, our progress in medical science, our ability to fly around the globe, the World Wide Web that connects us all—yet our greatest advances are lacking one vital component. We have not given ourselves the tools that we need to spiritually or emotionally thrive in the world we have created. We are failing because we have advanced as humans at the cost of many of the things that we hold dear.

When we look at our individual realities, it's as though we have been trapped inside a microscopic world that we mistook for an expansive landscape. What we think is the whole world—vast and sprawling—

is actually just a microcosm of what we are capable of experiencing or contributing to. We operate from within this limitation, breathing in shallowly and fighting for air, believing we are taking a full breath. We think we see the world in full color, when what we see is actually shrouded in darkness. We move among shadows, believing them to be light.

What should be some of our most basic tools—being present in the moment, connecting with our hearts to one another, and showing compassion and care to those who have less fortune—have been lost in our scramble to do, be, and achieve more. Although it often feels catastrophic and hopeless, and as though we have reached the point of no return, the tools we have neglected are much more within our reach than we might think. And as was highlighted in the previous chapter: although many of these issues are reflected outside of us, everything changes when we begin to deal with them inside ourselves first.

## Cracking Our Worlds

In order for us to create the kind of change we are seeking on a global level, we need to be able to crack the outer shell of our personal world to fully let the light in. I call this outer shell the "egoskeleton." Similar to the exoskeleton of an insect or crustacean, this structure supports us through certain periods of our life development. As with the exoskeleton, at some point we outgrow it, and at that point, it needs to be shed. For an insect, this evolution is triggered by the physical growth of the organism, but for the egoskeleton, this growth is mentally induced. Failure to shed the exoskeleton will inhibit the growth of a crayfish in nature. In our case, if it is not shed, the egoskeleton will inhibit our growth. When we have the courage to start demolishing the egoskeleton of the limited and limiting world we exist in, we can transform any limited thinking, and more effectively contribute to change in our outer worlds. The key is that *we need to work on each of these aspects concurrently.* We transform our inner worlds so that we see through different eyes, and then we look outward and make our contribution from our new perspective.

Some of us have already realized that the evolution of our world starts with what lies within, and have taken steps to look inwards, making a slight crack in our world. Others have let some light into some corners of their lives, but haven't invited it to all areas yet. The truth is, many of us *believe* we have had our revelation, but are still living from a fraction of what is possible. There are those among us who preach a particular point of view and try to convert others, but there is no real substance to what is being taught. One of the things we must be ready to wake up to is the possibility that *we think our limited world has already cracked, but only a glimpse of light is currently showing through.* So as we progress, we need to constantly question our own limitations and be open to the fact that, although the landscape is shifting, there is still so much more for each of us to see.

## HOW WE CREATE THE CRACK

Understanding that we are trapped and cut off from true reality (and that there is another option) is the first crack in our egoskeleton. Having the courage to make that crack creates a catalyst for change moving forward.

The paradox is that although most human beings would say that they want to be free, it's almost universally true that *we don't want to take the steps required to make that happen.* Most of us would rather stay comfortable in that prison of the egoskeleton. Often it takes a knock from outside for the shell of our world to begin to break. We have a physical breakdown, our partner leaves us, we lose a fortune, someone we love dies. And then the limited ways we've been seeing the world are involuntarily dismantled for us.

If you've been fortunate enough to have had an experience in life that has jolted you awake, then half the battle has already been won. Yet to manufacture the crack with no knock from the outside takes great courage and confidence, because almost always, something has got to give for it to start. If you are locked tightly inside your shell, it's going to require at least one major life shift—and maybe a multitude of changes—before the world that feels like it is safe (but is actually limiting you) begins to fall apart. Part of that dismantling comes from admitting that you are clinging to certain pieces for comfort and familiarity—and being willing to let them go.

Whatever your destructive habits, however much you have convinced yourself that it is OK for them to take over, there is some part of you that knows that they are preventing you from experiencing true personal growth. There is likely something in you, even a tiny fraction, that hears these words and can feel something stir inside. Some part of you that knows that the "socially acceptable" thing you do, that you've been shrugging off for years, decades even (because everyone else does it, so it must be OK), is actually the thing that is eating you from the inside. It's the thing that steals your soul. You know it. But you likely don't want to face it. So you look around you, and you see everyone else doing something similar, and you tell yourself, "Well, that's just the way it is. I'm only human, after all." You shrug it off, joke about it, or even identify with it, but every now and then there is a voice in you that questions it. So far you have likely enjoyed the comfort that it brings way too much to really give that voice a chance. If you are willing, then here is where that changes.

For me, my egoskeleton was unbreakable for the longest period of time. I was running around blindly in this world, doing things that others around me considered "successful," and stacking up the praise from friends to strengthen my shell. It was only after all this running had left my tank on empty, and extreme burnout ensued, that my false support structure began to crumble. My marriage fell apart, I became involved in an affair which quickly turned ugly, my dad died, and my mom followed four months later. One by one, these events became the pestle and mortar that pulverized my egoskeleton into dust.

Part of my breakdown involved beginning to listen to the inner voice of wisdom and reason that I hadn't learned to connect to before. And part of the conscious revolution that we are presenting in this book is to get you intrigued enough by the potential of a new way of living, so that you start listening to that inner voice in yourself too. You dive in, and the crack in your own egoskeleton that you may have been avoiding begins to happen naturally, without you having to force it, or hopefully that happens before you create your own series of events that become the pestle and mortar that grind you down. Maybe you already have a sense that you are ready to crack in that way. You look at all the societal pressures, all the social media pressures, and the feeling that everything is closing in around you, this "doomsday" feeling that has been heightened by the media and that we have been collectively pulled into. Instead of being dragged down by the world

you are in, you choose to throw yourself into turning everything on its head and seeing it a different way.

In the next section of this chapter, we'll look at the different aspects of awakening from this dream.

## AWAKENING FROM OUR MESS

Our personal awakening starts in our mind with awareness of our thoughts and actions. When we fully understand this, and see the prisons that we have created in our mind and the way they limit our thoughts and actions, we can begin to break down the outer shell of our world so that we can operate in a more expansive way. The foundational components of this change are:

Awareness → Thoughts + Emotions → Awakening

## AWARENESS

A conscious revolution is the best hope for our current paradigm as a species, and accessing awareness is the most revolutionary thing you can do.

Present moment awareness is the binding agent of our existence. With it we can hold ourselves together in even the toughest of circumstances. Without it we crumble and fall apart, lost in the history of what has gone before or the fear of what might be. We've all been there, chewing on an old memory from the past, worrying about what's coming around the corner. Many of us spend a significant amount of the day engaged in this kind of thought. This "compulsive thinking" is so socially acceptable that it has seeped into the language of our culture. It's so commonplace to tell each other what we are fearing or what went wrong, that most of us don't question this constant attachment to regret about what has passed or the fear of what's to come.

Many of us have grown up in situations where awareness was not taught. In our homes, in our schools, in our societies around the globe, we were taught to operate from fear. The subtle way this is taught to us might be different in every household, or each individual society, but it has a common theme. It centers around some kind of threat to our survival. There is often an "us" that are the good ones and a "them" that is the threat. If you think about how much this hero and villain narrative has been sold to us in American society (and filtered down into the rest of the Western world), you will start to see it occurring in many different themes. In our superhero movies, in our movies in general, there is always a good and an evil. A right and a wrong. And this mentality, this mindset, trickles down into almost every issue that we collectively face.

This kind of mindset creates a subtle level of fear, which is the opposite of awareness. As we highlighted in chapter 1, when fear is triggered, it shuts down the higher centers of our brain so that we are no longer aware. We need to undo this teaching—so that we don't continuously operate from what we were taught as children—and discover how to undo some of the negative effects of growing up in a world that is driven by survival and fear.

Instead of being lost in the thought of what happened in the past, or what will happen in the future, we can combine the essence of all our experience into being here now. Now is the only time you will ever have to change your world on an individual and global level, and realizing this, not just on an intellectual level, but on a practical level, you can apply this knowing in every moment. *That's the kind of commitment it takes to live from a place of awareness.*

Many of the "spiritual" books out there will dress awareness up. It's made into something mystical and unreachable. My upbringing, my view on life, the way I show up, have made me see it, and experience it, as something much more practical. Remove all the fluff, and it's something that can start in this moment, right now, wherever you are.

**AWARENESS EXERCISE:** Step outside for a moment and slow down. Look around you, and focus on something really simple like a tree, a flower, a bicycle or car parked nearby or even an industrial building. Don't put a label on it. Just be in the space of seeing it for the first time. See the perfection of it without being in the story of how perfect it is. See if you can look around you with the same kind of eyes, and without any preconceptions or narratives about what you see. Look at yourself in the bigger picture of the universe, as an individual with a point of view, moving through time and space. Grasp that intellectually while simultaneously letting it go. Just look around, observing the beauty that's presenting itself to you, without judgment. That's awareness.

Discovering awareness can be unsettling, especially for those of us who have been locked so tightly in the dream. It can feel like finding yourself in outer space, just floating. Nothing to hold on to, nothing to ground you. This can make you feel aimless and alone.

When I began to experience awareness, it went something like this. Before I had any real awareness, I felt as though I was connected to everything, but in a dreamlike way. When I realized my illusion of connection was not real, and I started to see through the eyes of awareness, suddenly I did feel that aloneness, like there was nothing to connect to. Many people panic at this stage, and "get lost in the void," but if you can get past that feeling, there is a third stage to this process, and for me it was when I became connected to everything—but this time, in reality, rather than in a dream.

When you feel fully connected to reality, you have a totally different interpretation of your surroundings. You can read the signs from your own body, and from others' too. You can better navigate your ups and downs. Life has a much more natural rhythm. When you get used to living in the space of awareness, you finally get to know your real self as opposed to operating mainly from behind a mask or a learned identity. You can respond to people quickly and at a gut level, beyond reacting to them. Relationships may still have their challenges, but you are able to navigate them more easily. This includes your business, your work, and your personal relationships.

Beyond your relationships, there is something deeper when you engage with awareness. There's something there. Another dimension, that is not there when you are operating unaware. It's a space of unlimited potential. It makes everything you're doing a little more interesting. Even if that everything is brushing your teeth, or washing the dishes, or binding a report, or waiting on the bus, (or in my case, hiking a mile through the woods to do a bat exit count for the ninety-seventh time), you are totally there. You're content to be there in that space, in that moment, whatever you're doing. You're fully into whatever task you're performing—more fully even than the first time you ever did it—and with this comes a freshness and aliveness that cannot be manufactured.

> **Thinking Point:** If you were raised in the Western world, you live in a culture where you were trained that your identity comes from everything you have gathered, gained, and achieved. Try flipping it on its head. Ask yourself, "What would I be if they stripped everything away from me? My job, my friends, my thoughts, my emotions, my identity, my house, my car. What would I be?" See if you can get a sense of yourself, your presence, your unadulterated perfection without the things that you've been taught to identify with.

## THOUGHTS

## YOU ARE NOT YOUR THOUGHTS

> 99 *A human being [...] experiences himself, his thoughts and feelings as something separated from the rest—a kind of optical delusion of his consciousness.*
> **Albert Einstein**

The first shot fired in this conscious revolution occurs when you understand that you are not your thoughts.

Once awareness starts to become more consistent, you'll notice, more and more, the mechanism that is keeping you from living consistently in the moment—a mechanism that continuously sucks you into the past or catapults you into the future. That mechanism is thought. The irony is, you cannot create revolution if you are in your head thinking about revolution.

Our greatest freedom comes when we truly understand that our thoughts and worries are not real things, but that we allow them to control us to the point of distress. Most of us don't realize that this is a choice. Our cultural training has taught us to identify so completely with our thoughts that we believe that we are them. Most people's reality is a continuous loop of the past and the future. This learned behavior of allowing ourselves to be pulled in all different directions by our thoughts—combined with the more recent distractions of modern technology—keeps us locked away in a mind prison that can be difficult to escape from, largely because we don't really see another option. Earlier I talked about the crack in the shell of your world. The key to life is to get your "shell cracked" and move beyond your illusory thoughts into a space of single moment awareness. Reality then becomes the space between the thoughts and stories you're telling yourself, instead of the thoughts themselves.

In an iconic speech, Jim Carey shared:

> *A few months ago [...] I woke up and I suddenly got it. I understood, suddenly, how thought was just an illusory thing, and how thought is responsible for, if not all, most of the suffering we experience. And then I suddenly felt that I was looking at these thoughts from*

*another perspective, and I thought, 'Who is it that is aware that I'm thinking?' Suddenly, I was thrown into this expansive, amazing feeling of freedom —from myself, from my problems. I saw that I was bigger than what I do, bigger than my body, everything and everyone.*[1]

I know what Jim Carey was talking about at the start of his quote: when I was building my company Apogee, I began to notice something similar: it was never reality that actually impacted me. Losing a major client, having a key member of staff who was crucial to a major project quit at short notice—dealing with these, or similar challenges in the moment rarely had an impact. What did impact me was the torture of my illusory thoughts of what might happen in the future.

## Operating From Conscious Thought

You likely picked this book up because you heard about how Artemes has a mission to make a positive impact in the world. Many of us envision a world of peace, but it has often been said that world peace can only follow self peace. We have to strip away the layers of thoughts and ideas we have in our heads to get to the core of this peace. When we try to create beauty outside of ourselves, yet we are still tortured by our thoughts, what we create is from within the limitations of our own pain. So the first step is to reach in, to see those thoughts, and to realize them for what they are. When millions of us start to adjust ourselves in this way, that's when we will start to grow a healthy and conscious society. We are making society better for all by making things better within, and with this adjusted perspective, we can then ask what we can do to support the greater whole. These two components together are key. Because you can be the most heart-centered person in the world but how does that help the world, unless you are prepared to act on behalf of others too? Some of the modern spiritual movements have been way too focused on the journey of the self. With our work at Artemes, we focus on both. We move spirituality out of "I, me, and mine," and into the paradigm of looking within, making adjustments, and then, from this place, reaching out to the world with solutions and new perspectives.

Within each of us is the potential for greatness and peacefulness. And there is also the potential for terribleness and hate. When we realize that most of these potentials begin with our thoughts, and most of these thoughts are ones we have been trained to think, we can have a greater impact on our reality. We don't just dance to the sound of the thoughts that we think. We stop. We interrupt. We bring consciousness to that which enters our mind. We question. We disrupt.

Oftentimes we hear about someone who broke out of their destructive conditioning. "This woman was a Nazi but she started to see the world through different eyes," "This guy was a sexist, then he started to develop respect for women," "This woman was in a religious cult but she found her way out." We love these stories as humans, not just because they represent an end to prejudice, but also because they represent an end to programming. We love to hear that someone saw through the limitations of their reality, and stopped behaving in programmed impulses, to become so much more.

If you can step back and observe your thoughts and avoid moments of instantaneous reactions, you can really start to see how your reality is

constructed. As you'll see if you take the Artemes Training in the third part of this book, that pause before you react is something we are going to build on more and more. What we are doing in that pause is building genuine compassion. In that pause, anyone—including a religious fundamentalist or a neo-Nazi—can shift. That pause to recognize thought can create a chain reaction that spreads out in every direction. If we all take responsibility for that here, in this moment, who knows what our chain reaction can create in the next five, ten or twenty years.

## EMOTIONS

Often our thoughts alone have no power to disrupt. We can think thousands of thoughts in a day, and although it wastes mental energy and keeps us out of the moment, spiraling in the whirlpool of our mind, nothing actually changes. It's when our thoughts trigger an emotional response that we tend to spiral out of control. When we think a thought that relates to a challenging experience we went through, it can trigger a cascade of emotions that takes us out of the present.

This trigger is actually a survival response that is trying to keep us safe. We are designed to protect ourselves from re-experiencing anything that has been a threat to us in the past. If something in our external world reminds us of that threat, a similar emotion to the one we experienced in the past is triggered to remind us to keep ourselves safe. The trouble is that this system often triggers when we are not actually in threat. We spiral into an escalating cycle of emotions and find ourselves reacting from that place, even when this response hurts more than it helps.

# AWAKENING

Once we learn to disrupt our thoughts enough to see their illusory nature, and rewrite our emotional responses so that we aren't experiencing everything as a threat, we begin to awaken from the limitations of what we have learned. Again, many spiritual teachings will give this some kind of elevated status. From where I stand, it is just me—minus the lies that I was told and the fears that I learned, that I bought into as truth.

I was forty years old before I woke up to the misperceptions and lies that had shaped my reality. My crack in the shell came when my life broke down, knocking me into a different reality. I lived a repeatable dream of work and parties for ten straight years, and I'm not sure if it was exhaustion or boredom that finally caused me to crack. I burned out and broke. As I've shared, I had an affair and my marriage died. The community that I had worked so hard to build fell apart. My parents died. My ego died. And out of this, my true self emerged.

I had to crash and burn and rebuild from there. From where I see the world now, everything is always as it should be. All the hurts that I have received, and all the hurts that I have given, have slowly faded into the background. They have not disappeared altogether and I still own and take responsibility for all that I have said and done, and the impact that has had on the ones I love. The salty and bitter tastes still linger somewhere, but I have made my peace with all that has gone before.

What happened to me was pretty standard and it can occur for anyone. I say that, not to trivialize my experience, but just because in many spiritual circles, "waking up from the dream" is sold as some big deal reserved for the few. Personally, I don't agree. My sense is that we all have the opportunity within us to crack through our shell, and to take that opportunity to shake awake and take action in a whole new way. In our popular culture, there have been many references to this opportunity. In the movie *Joe versus the Volcano*, Joe wakes up to life for the first time and demands others around him look at how they are sleeping through a miserable life because they have been programmed to do so. In an iconic scene where he quits his job, he recognizes the fear that's been keeping him asleep:

*Joe: You look terrible, Mr. Waturi. You look like a bag of shit stuffed in a cheap suit. Not that anyone could look good under these zombie lights. I can feel them sucking the juice out of my eyeball. Suck, suck, suck, SUCK... [makes a sucking noise] For 300 bucks a week, that's the news. For 300 bucks a week, I've lived in this sink, this used rubber.*

*Mr. Waturi: You watch it, mister! There's a woman here!*

*Joe: Don't you think I know that, Frank? Don't you think I am aware there is a woman here? I can smell her, like, like a flower. I can taste her, like sugar on my tongue. When I'm twenty feet away I can hear the fabric of her dress when she moves in her chair. Not that I've done anything about it. I've gone all day, every day, not doing, not saying, not taking the chance, for 300 bucks a week, and Frank, the coffee stinks, it's like arsenic. The lights give me a headache. If the lights don't give you a headache, you must be dead; let's arrange the funeral.*

*Mr. Waturi: You better get outta here right now! I'm telling you!*

***Joe:*** *You're telling me nothing. And why, I ask myself, why have I put up with you? I can't imagine, but now I know. Fear. Yellow freakin' fear. I've been too chickenshit afraid to live my life, so I sold it to you for 300 freakin' dollars a week! You're lucky I don't kill you! You're lucky I don't rip your freakin' throat out! But I'm not going to! And maybe you're not so lucky at that. 'Cause I'm gonna leave you here, Mr. Wahoo Waturi, and what could be worse than that?*

This scene represents that moment that maybe you've had already or maybe is yet to come, where you just realize that the dance you've been dancing is not actually real. And in a contrasting part of the film, the character Patricia tells Joe:

> *My father says almost the whole world's asleep. Everybody you know, everybody you see, everybody you talk to. He says only a few people are awake. And they live in a state of constant, total amazement.*

That state is the one we are opening to as we progress with Artemes so that it can be available to everyone and not just the select few, as Patricia's father highlighted has been the case so far. And from that place, you will make your impact on humanity, with your eyes wide open.

## SUMMING UP

In this chapter we touched upon how one of the biggest challenges that humanity faces exists within each and every one of us.

### We looked at:

- How our greatest advances are lacking one vital component. We have not given ourselves the tools that we need to spiritually or emotionally thrive in the world we have created.

- What should be some of our most basic tools—being present in the moment, connecting with our hearts to one another, and showing compassion and care to those who have less fortune— have been lost in our scramble to do, be, and achieve more.

- How, if we are to create the kind of change we are seeking on a global level, we need to be able to crack the egoskeleton of our personal world to fully let the light in.

- How having the courage to start demolishing the egoskeleton of the limited world we exist in will enable us to transform any limited thinking, and more effectively contribute to change in our outer worlds too.

- Understanding that we are trapped and cut off from true reality (and that there is another option) is the first crack we can make in our egoskeleton.

- How it's almost universally true that *we don't want to take the steps required to* crack open our egoskeleton.

- How our personal awakening starts in our mind with awareness of our thoughts and actions.

- The summary of the path to this realization, which is Awareness → Thoughts + Emotions → Awakening
  - **Awareness:** Bringing consciousness to every individual moment
  - **Thoughts:** Understanding that we are not our thoughts
  - **Emotions:** Recognizing the trigger of emotions that take us out of the present
  - **Awakening:** Awakening from the limitations of what we have learned.

In the chapter that follows, we'll look at what we need to begin to do to clean up this mess on a personal and global level. Then in Part Two of this book we will introduce the unique system of Artemes so that you can contribute to a dynamic, new solution to the challenges we collectively face.

# CHAPTER THREE
## CLEANING UP OUR MESS

Before diving into the Artemes System, we need to define the different kinds of challenges we are facing. Many of us have started to repeat the collective beliefs that "The world is on fire," or "We've left it too late," and while there are very real and immediate challenges at hand, with much that needs to be done, our approach with Artemes is a very practical one. We each work towards clearing up our individual patterns and programs that are keeping us locked in old ways of thinking and behaving, while simultaneously picking an area— whether it's social, political or environmental—that we feel most aligned with, and bringing forward our efforts to create change.

This chapter takes a practical overview of the different types of messes we have collectively created, so that you can pick your area of passion, and combine your own growth journey with igniting your purpose to create change.

## PERSONAL MESS

It's already been highlighted that we begin by looking within at our own personal mess before we start looking outwards. This is because we want to make our contribution to humanity from beyond our fears, programs, and reactions—from a place where we are level-headed, conscious, and awake. If we don't make this switch first, we operate from within the collective soup of catastrophic thinking, where we worry that the human race, or the earth, is not going to make it, and we act out of survival rather than from a place of consciousness. When we are operating from survival, we are much more likely to go into the attack and defend mindset. Yet when we operate from a more conscious state, we look at the world and the people in it with a greater sense of unity, compassion, and understanding. When we address the challenges of the world from this place, it is less out of fear of a catastrophic future and more because we want to create a fairer, more connected, and compassionate world.

When it comes to clearing up our personal mess, many spiritual paths stop there—and stay there. If we are not careful, we get stuck in a never-ending loop of sorting out our own challenges. In the Artemes Training, the point of sorting out our personal mess is so that we can have not only an incredible connected life, but that we can also go on to do something useful for others with that life. Whether you dedicate yourself to transforming social or political issues, deeply caring for others, or impacting the environment, once

you have begun to work with your personal mess, you can have more impact in the world.

Our personal mess is something we've learned and built up over time. For most of us, it started when we were children. Modern psychology often points to our parents, blaming them for what we've become, but they themselves were operating from the same cycle of pain that was passed onto them, and that they passed onto us. Just as their own parents did to them, our parents gave off an energy that was reflected within us. If there is nervousness, hunger, or anxiety in our mother's eyes, we will reflect this in our internal space. If our father connects to us with anger or with pain, so too do we learn to operate from that which we have been taught. We learn to feel the emotions that our parents are experiencing, and although it is often not their intention, we become a product of our upbringing as a result. One of the first layers of the shell of our world that we need to begin to crack is the layer of who we believe we are, based on all the limitations that we learned before.

## SOCIAL MESS

Our society is currently at a breaking point. We are conditioned to be lost in material goals, and are far more obsessed with how we look on the surface than being the master of our own internal climate.

The challenge is that when the individual struggles, society struggles too. Although we humans have the potential to thrive as societies, we have collectively lost our way—our current social conditioning puts thin filters of judgment, rules, and morals over the reality of our world.

This social layer, comprised of all of these filters, creates a seemingly impenetrable one that is often difficult to identify. We can't see it, and no one around us can see it, because we're all seeing that one, opaque, layer. With every rule, with every lie, with every limitation, the layer around our personal world grows thicker. Instead of participating in a healthy and integrated society where we feel part of a greater whole, we begin to think of ourselves as separate and distinct from the outside world, trapped and cut off from our true existence, thrashing around, angst-ridden, trying to make sense of who we are and figure out the point of all this. And so the layer thickens and we never truly breathe the air or feel the sunlight on our skin.

We experience all kinds of mistruths and protective behaviors. If this system has quashed us, we don't want to admit that it is the case. Nobody wants to think that they were duped or lied to their whole life. So we defend whatever we have, because it's often easier to hold tight to a lie than to face the truth of what we have been sold.

In *The End of Poverty*, Jeffrey D. Sachs challenges the derogatory misbelief that others are poor because they are lazy or stupid. "Virtually every society that was once poor has been castigated for being lazy and unworthy until its citizens became rich, at which point, their new wealth was 'explained' by their industriousness." He later goes on to highlight that arguments of this nature hold two main problems. Firstly, that "cultures change with economic times and circumstances," and secondly, that cultural interpretations are "usually made on the basis of prejudice rather than measurable evidence."[1] We need to stop pigeonholing those with socio-economic challenges so that we can build a system that is fairer to all.

Where I was born, we were all stamped as losers, abusers or drug addicts. Not fit for contributing to American society. We didn't see options before us. Many of the friends I grew up with had long stints in jail or are dead now. My mother had to support us by selling drugs, and as a child, I remember the smell of marijuana plants in our house. Later on, my mother was sent to prison—not because she was a bad human being, but because she wanted to protect and nourish us, and give us a chance to become something greater than she was. She was doing her best with the resources that she had, but it wasn't a reason that is socially acceptable in American society. For trying to make the best of a difficult situation, she was thrown into prison where she remained for two years. This system of ours is not one with eyes—it is blinded by the pursuit of individualism and personal greed. Huge corporations can get away with pushing Oxycontin for mass profit, yet my mom went to jail for selling marijuana because she wanted to feed her kids.

With my eyes open now, I can see how people with no choices are forced down a tough path in order to make ends meet. If they go against the rules of society, for whatever reason, they can be locked up for a long time.

Or, they live from paycheck to paycheck (if they are lucky enough to have a job). They do the best they can. And they defend themselves against anything that's going to take that away from them.

Despite the challenges around me, as a child I was fortunate to be able to see through some of the lies I had been told. There was something inside me that decided early on that I was going to step out of the role

I had been given. I lived in the "holler" in East Kentucky. Society had a label for us. They called us "holler rats." It's one of those labels that gets used for areas of socio-economic challenges in the same way that the derogatory term "trailer trash" gets used. Once you get labeled like that, your brain starts to wire in a way that means there is no escape. Somehow, my brain was firing differently. I remember telling myself at seven years old, "I'm never going to give in to this." I looked at the people around me dealing and early on I understood that they were doing so because they didn't see another way. For myself I could see something different. That feeling was always in the background, whatever I did.

When I was in eighth grade, a teacher came to me and said, "I've seen your test scores. I would love for you to be on the Quick Recall and Academic Team." Senior year we finished third in the state. Most importantly, that got me out of the holler so I could see another world. We would go around the region playing games. I saw Nashville, and other regions that were different from mine. Getting out of the holler helped me see a wider vision of the potential of the world.

I guess my teacher was a catalyst for shifting my perspective on the limitations of the world. She was thinking of my well-being. Yet one of the challenges of the social divides we've looked at is that those who benefit from having more, often aren't motivated to work towards the well-being of all. Especially in the US, survival-of-the-fittest culture, it is socially acceptable to divide our world into the haves and the have nots. With Artemes, we are aiming to create a more socially fair climate for us all.

Particularly in the US, when we start talking about fairer societies, some people immediately respond with the label of socialism. What we are doing with Artemes, however, is closer to altruistic capitalism. It's easy to assume that altruistic capitalism is just benefiting those who have financial challenges, but it's actually an approach that is essential to our thriving as a whole.

We have to collectively challenge the paradigm of winners and losers in our society before our world heads towards a version of reality where there are only a few in power. The Artemes System that follows in Part Two of this book is one of the ways we can contribute to breaking up that paradigm.

## ECONOMIC MESS

*Once we give ourselves social permission to think that money, not love, is the organizing principle of a well-adjusted society, chaos is inevitable.[2]*
**Marianne Williamson**

Our social and our economic messes exist side by side, and we can't separate one from the other. Economic disparity is the linchpin that sits at the center of most issues of inequality. As intersectionality has become an increasingly utilized buzzword, the quest to find the places where each issue of inequality meets has become a hot topic. Economic disparity, however, seems to sit at the center of almost every issue. We can't talk about racial equality, prison reform, equal pay rights for women, immigration, or refugee equality, for example, without touching on the issue of socio-economic gaps. However, there are some aspects of the economic mess that we need to draw out separately so we can understand and address the full spectrum of the challenges that we collectively face.

When I picture times of old, when our forefathers landed in what we now call the US, I always imagine that the socio-economic gaps were much greater than they are now. Yet inequality on a global level is an issue that has become more prevalent in the last 200 years. In economics, the term "GDP per capita" means taking the total money that a country makes and then dividing it into how many people live there. In 1820, the richest nation in the world was the United Kingdom. If we measure its GDP per capita for that year, it was making only four times more than the poorest nation in the world, which was Africa.[3] (The study that we looked at referred to Africa as a nation as, in 1820, Africa was not defined by independent and separate countries, but rather colonies of superpowers seen as one nation.)

In 1998, the richest economy in the world (by then, the United States) had a GDP per capita twenty times that of the poorest nation (which was still Africa).[4]

Within twenty years, (1998 to the end of 2017), this ratio had increased to thirty-eight times, which shows that the global inequality rate is increasing at an unprecedented rate.

As of 2018, the eight richest people in the world had the equivalent wealth of the bottom 50 percent of the world (which means that eight people had the wealth of 3.6 billion people).[5]

In the US, while the average income for the bottom 60 percent of society has decreased in the last ten years, according to census data, the income of the top 10 percent has increased significantly. Moreover, between 1980 and 2009, the share of income for the top 10 percent increased from 33 percent to nearly 50 percent of all income.[6]

Among all the developed countries, the US, unbelievably, has one of the largest disparities between rich and poor (the only developed countries with a larger disparity are Chile, Uruguay and Singapore).[7]

## The Changing Face of Economics

In the last chapter we laid out why the economic game that humanity is currently playing is not the fairest to all. Many of us are asking, "What sort of rules do we need if we want a new game to be played?"

In an ideal world, all the basic needs of everyone born human would be taken care of. Our rights in such a world would include access to food, clean water, protection from the elements, and healthcare, at the very least. To have comfort and no fear is something that would ideally be a given for each human on this planet. By simply being human, you would basically win the universal lottery.

Today, we have a winner-loser mentality that says that "those people" need to work for what they get. That "they" need to pull themselves up by their bootstraps. Yet it is only a belief—not a necessary truth—that humans must work (and it seems that robots are soon going to be doing most of the work for us).

So, what would the benefit be of creating a game where the rules inherently took care of everyone? This was a question that was asked in a study led by Alessandro Pluchino at the University of Catania, Italy.[8] Pluchino et al. created a computer model of human talent and then set out to conduct experiments to see how talent and chance (i.e., luck) influenced performance.

For one experiment, Pluchino was interested in how funding priorities could potentially create different results in the scientific research community. Funding was distributed in one of three ways:

1. It was distributed equally to all scientists
2. It was randomly distributed to a subset of the scientists
3. It was distributed to scientists who had performed the best in the past.

The study tested which group performed best. Surprisingly, it wasn't the third group (that had performed best in the past), but the first group—those where funding was distributed equally—that performed best.

I'm guessing that if we took all the individuals in the world, divided them into three distinct groups, and then distributed resources to them in a similar way to what Pluchino did with the scientists, we would see similar results. What we see in our current game is that funding is distributed to those who have performed well in the past. This means that nearly 2 billion of the creative individuals in this world (the 36 percent that live in extreme poverty) are shackled by poverty and unable to take part in the game.[9]

What would happen if everyone in the world was set free to be creative? What would happen if no one had to worry about saving for their kid's education, or having healthcare when they retire, or having access to clean drinking water? What would happen if, like those lucky ones born financially stable, this pressure went away?

We can see an example of this through a test conducted in India.[10] Over an eighteen-month period, 6,000 individuals who were living below the poverty line were given small monthly income supplements. The results were not surprising.

Villages spent more on food and healthcare, children's school performance improved in 68 percent of families, personal savings tripled, and new business start-ups doubled. The study also observed an increase in economic activity, an improvement in housing and sanitation, improved nutrition, less food poverty, improved health, greater inclusion of the disabled in society, and a lack of frivolous spending.[11] Similar results have been shown in parallel studies.

We need to consider what would happen if the socio-economic pressures, particularly those of survival, no longer existed. What would our human potential be if we played the game this way? You can likely envision the type of world we would live in if human beings were more free to play an equal game.

In order to better understand wealth generation and redistribution, we first need to grasp the changing features of attitudes in economics as a whole.

From an economic perspective, inequality used to be seen as a humanitarian and philanthropic issue. In fact, in the old paradigm of economics, it was believed that addressing inequality would reduce economic growth; but now there is a new paradigm of economics—as well as a large amount of accompanying statistics—that argues the opposite.

The old paradigm said that the money that circulates in an economy can be shown as a pie, and what society should focus on is *expanding the size of the pie rather than focusing on the size of the piece that each person gets.* The argument was that if the whole pie size increases, the size of the slice that each person gets increases automatically too. It was also believed that focusing on the size of the pie slices detracts from working on increasing the size of the pie as a whole.

The new paradigm claims that working on increasing the size of the whole pie and working on fairness of the slices of the pie are not contradictory to one another. The new paradigm even goes further to claim that if the slices of pie are too unevenly distributed, it prevents the whole pie from increasing in size. *So the new paradigm in economics is leaning towards more fairness for all.*

Billionaire Ray Dalio shared his thoughts on this pie in a groundbreaking 2019 article that suggested we need a reformation in capitalism:

> *I think that most capitalists don't know how to divide the economic pie well and most socialists don't know how to grow it well, yet we are now at a juncture in which either a) people of different ideological inclinations will work together to skillfully re-engineer the system so that the pie is both divided and grown well or b) we*

*will have great conflict and some form of revolution that will hurt*
*most everyone and will shrink the pie.¹²*

In an interview with *Fox Business*'s Gerry Baker, Dalio shared that, "We can't take the existence of capitalism for granted." He also envisioned: "I think you could easily have a movement to an opposite extreme."

Although Dalio has been personally successful in the financial world, he has also criticized capitalism because of its inequalities. While he is a self-proclaimed capitalist, in the interview he also admitted, "If it's not working for the majority of people, it's not successful."

In the same interview, he proposed, "The key is you have to both increase the size of the pie through productivity and effective economic policies—and divide the pie well."

He also discussed leveling the playing field, asking, "Can we try for equal opportunity?" and "Can we measure how well we're doing on that?" and further, "Can we realize that the system is in jeopardy … unless we do that?"¹³

Similar sentiments were also shared by billionaire Marc Benioff, the CEO of Salesforce. When asked in an interview for *The Verge* by Casey Newton why there was an upsurge of so many tech companies, and why "tech workers are getting a sense of their own power," Benioff shared:

*I think they realized that we need a new capitalism—that capitalism*
*as we know it is dead, they have the ability to be part of the new*
*capitalism, and that means that they can bring their values to work.*

*These values can create value for them and for the companies they work for. And that businesses have to move this new capitalism—a more fair and equal sustainable way of doing business, that values all stakeholders as well as shareholders. And one of those key stakeholders is the employees themselves.[14]*

Nobel Prize winner in Economics, Joseph Stiglitz, who is one of the most prominent economists in the world, also identifies some of the challenges with our current system. He highlights that in a society with significant economic inequality, not all the money circulates. This is because the wealthy don't spend their money as much as the less affluent (because those with less money need to spend their income in order to live). So when money is circulating, it brings more economic growth to a society.

Therefore, tackling inequality makes sense from both a human and an economics perspective (and we will be looking at the how of this in Part Two of this book).

## Taking Individual Financial Responsibility

Although much of this chapter has focused on the systems that we need to disrupt in order to create change, it's essential that we take responsibility for our individual choices and how they contribute to the whole. The first two chapters discussed the different ways we check out and fall asleep, and these are also reflected in our financial choices.

In *A Politics of Love*, Marianne Williamson eloquently highlights the version of reality that we have been sold so that we are easier to market to. She shares:

> *Self-love has become an odd sort of god in America. A generation that has become so sensitive to its own pain is often desensitized to the pain of others. One would think Jesus had come to earth to say, "Love yourself." Somewhere along the line, the "Love each other," "Love your neighbor as yourself" part has been subtly minimized, conveniently so for a market-based system that legitimizes self-centeredness as a lead-in to "I absolutely have to have this."*[15]

If we look around us, it is easy to focus on the maldistribution of wealth, particularly in a capitalist society. When I share that, according to the Borgen Project—an organization that fights global poverty—it would take $30 billion a year to end world hunger, most people's first response is to look to those who have the greatest proportion of the wealth to fix the problem.[16] As of March 2019:

- Jeff Bezos of Amazon has a net worth of $131 billion
- Bill Gates has a net worth of $96.5 billion
- Warren Buffett, Berkshire Hathaway CEO, has a net worth of $82.5 billion.[17]

It's easy to place the solution to the world hunger crisis on the billionaires of the world, and indeed it seems that individually or collectively, they could solve the problem—and there is a commonly held belief that those with the greatest power should take the most responsibility. It's equally easy to put responsibility on the government. For example, the US defense budget is $737 billion per year. Just a fraction of this could potentially solve the world hunger crisis, let alone address the problems of the hungry in the US, where, in 2016, 41 million people struggled with hunger issues.[18]

However, when we blame those with power for the shortfalls of society, we simultaneously give our own power away, because what we do individually is equally important. With the Artemes System, we are not simply looking outside of ourselves to point blame at the government or underscore the unfair distribution of wealth. Instead we are asking questions, such as "What can we do on the ground?" "What is our role in socially impacting these challenges?" "How do we rally the people that we influence to make small, but vital, differences at a grassroots level?"

When we look at our mass expenditure, we can see some of the different ways we've chosen to check out of being responsible for the whole:

- The total pet industry expenditure for 2015 in the US was $60.59 billion[19] and globally in 2016 it topped over $100 billion worldwide.[20] The average young person from Generation Z spends around $71 for holiday gifts[21] for their pet.
- Beauty is a $445 billion industry.[22]
- The global fashion industry is valued at $3 trillion.[23]
- On Cyber Monday, (*one day*) in 2017, Americans spent $6.59 billion.[24] The following year, 2018, they spent $7.9 billion.[25]

These figures help us to understand that society has far more financial power to collectively make an impact than we might realize, and that much of our work is about creating new systems, rather than waiting for changes to come from above.

# POLITICAL MESS

Our socio-economic mess is often reinforced by the political systems of our individual countries. As we wake up from our social mess, we realize that those in positions of power benefit from keeping us small. If we are lost in fear, or worry, if we are distracted by materialism and always chasing more, those in power will benefit most, because we are more valuable to the system when we are fully operating within its limitations, than when we are free to think for ourselves.

With my eyes wide open, I can see the way that leaders of this nature (and they exist in many political parties) manipulate language to create and keep power. It is easy to blame those who voted for a leader such as Trump when we find him in power. The truth is, his carefully articulated campaign, based on data science,[26] was designed to manipulate those who were already in survival mode to give away further power, on the promise that he would solve the many issues that had triggered them into survival in the first place. As Gore Vidal shares in *History of the National Security State*, "I'd say the average American is a very peaceful sort of person, rather very shrewd about his [her/their] own interests." He highlights that this is "why we have created advertising genius," which we have invented "to get him [her/them] to vote against his [her/their] own interest time after time again."[27]

This is how those who currently hold the power inch the world further and further into the direction where their power increases. How this happens is never really taught to you in school. I had some outstanding teachers who rooted for us to move beyond the current paradigm, but mostly the system was rigged against me. I was taught

American history, and why we are better than the English, and some math, and a bit of science. But I wasn't really taught about the system that subjugated me or why I was piss-poor in the first place.

To break down these political structures, we need leaders who are willing to both embrace and solve social challenges. Andrew Yang, 2020 Democratic presidential candidate, was one such example of a political figure willing to challenge these structures. After working as an entrepreneur in the Midwest of the US, and witnessing firsthand the socio-economic decay, he proposed a Universal Basic Income—or Freedom Dividend—where each US citizen would receive $1000 per month. This is a prime example of how a political system can dramatically impact a social structure. (The challenge for Yang was that his efforts were focused on changing the system from within an already corrupted paradigm. It is a contrast to what we are doing with Artemes, in that we are creating a system outside the current paradigm.)

For the US, where healthcare is not a given, where someone can get sick and lose everything, where social security is barely existent and where homelessness is on the rise in all major cities, this kind of radical innovation is what is needed to overhaul the winner-loser mentality which comes with the American identity.

## ENVIRONMENTAL MESS

When humanity is cut off from its true nature, this disconnect reflects in the wider world around us. The environmental issues that are created by those who are in a state of disconnection are a reflection of this issue. If we look at the issue from the outside, it makes perfect sense that if we

went astray from ourselves, we also went astray from what is inherently best for the human race and the world as a whole. Our global wealth has been concentrated in the hands of a few companies that, for the most part, are led by unmindful practices that are centered on profit and greed. These corporations cut corners, with communities and the environment bearing the weight of their success. This is a global race to the bottom in which all participants eventually lose.

Part of the disconnect is that we, as individuals and individual countries, don't take responsibility for the whole. When we think of environmental issues, we talk about "Brazil's problem" or "Australia's problem." Yet it is humanity's issue that the rain forests of Brazil have been depleted, and not simply an issue for Brazil alone. Similarly, the issue with the Great Barrier Reef of Australia is humanity's to deal with. The loss of the Great Barrier Reef would be a loss for all of us, not just for Australia alone. We must get beyond our nationalistic point of view that "This is mine. That belongs to you," so we can solve these issues collectively.

If we, the countries of the world, are going to approach this existence as a game where each is a competitor, it is going to be an ugly race to the bottom. Many of the First World countries have risen to the top by exploiting not only their own resources, but the resources of the entire world. Other countries see what these exploitative countries have and naturally want some of it themselves. Knowing this, the First World countries must come to the aid of the rest of the world, helping them in such a way that the diverse ecosystems of the world are not destroyed. I see this in my work as a trained bat biologist, specializing in threatened and endangered species. Since 2006, millions of bats have been killed by a fungus-induced malady called White-nose Syndrome

(WNS). The fungus kills the bats by aggravating them to such a degree that they wake up repeatedly during hibernation. Waking up for the bats requires a substantial energy output that they must make up or die. The bats are either forced to exit the cave at inopportune times (during a hike in early March 2019, I observed a bat foraging during the daytime and soon thereafter being preyed upon by a hawk) or they simply die asleep in hibernation.

Insects, the main prey of the echolocation-specific bat species, are also being decimated. A recent comprehensive review of studies showing insect declines estimated that 40 percent of these insects are potentially headed for extinction within the next decade or two.[28] The authors posit that if this situation continues it could lead to widespread ecosystem failure.

The bat situation will not be fixed by humanity's current state of consciousness. Neither will the insect situation be fixed by the current state of consciousness. Environmental issues will continue to degrade until humans reach a level of understanding that is inclusive of all the species on this planet.

I truly believe that this is our collective turning point. For this to happen, it is the youngest among us who must champion these ideas and lead. Leaders such as Greta Thunberg, who started her activism career at fifteen years old. At the United Nations General Assembly in 2019 she told the audience, "Right here, right now is where we draw the line. The world is waking up. And change is coming, whether you like it or not." The younger generation can see beyond the socially-constructed greed. We need to take their counsel forward so that we can effect lasting change.

## SUMMING UP

The challenges that we collectively face show up on an individual, social, and global level.

### We summarize these challenges into:

### PERSONAL MESS

- In the Artemes Training, we sort out our personal mess so that we can have an incredible connected life and so that we can also go on to do something useful for others with that life.

- When it comes to clearing up our personal mess, many spiritual paths stop there—and stay there. If we are not careful, we get stuck in a never-ending loop of sorting out our own challenges.

### SOCIAL MESS

- Particularly in the US, when we start talking about fairer societies, some people immediately respond, labeling it as socialism. What we are doing with Artemes, however, is closer to altruistic capitalism.

- When the individual struggles, society struggles too.

- We often can't see through our social conditioning, because the layers surrounding us are so thick.

## ECONOMIC MESS

- Economic disparity is the linchpin that sits at the center of most issues of inequality.

- We need to create a fairer game where the rules inherently take care of everyone.

- We also need to take an honest look at our own financial behaviors, and how they are contributing to the challenges we collectively face.

## POLITICAL MESS

- Our socio-economic mess is often reinforced by the political systems of our individual countries.

- As we wake up from our social mess, we realize that those in positions of power benefit from keeping us small.

## ENVIRONMENTAL MESS

- When humanity is cut off from its true nature, this disconnect is reflected in the wider world around us.

- The environmental issues that are created by those who are in a state of disconnection are a reflection of this issue.

- Part of the disconnect is that we, as individuals and individual countries, don't take responsibility for the whole.

● We need to effect lasting change, and be guided by the younger generation who can see beyond the socially-constructed greed.

Now that we have touched the surface of the interconnectedness of the issues we collectively face, in the chapter that follows, we'll introduce the unique system of Artemes, so you can begin contributing to cleaning up these challenges.

**ARTEMES**
A Conscious Economic System for Creating
Equality in an Unbalanced World

# ARTEMES SYSTEM

The Artemes System consists of two components: Aware Leadership and Conscious Cryptocurrency.

# CHAPTER FOUR

## AWARE LEADERSHIP

*" You never change things by fighting the existing reality. To change something, build a new model that makes the existing model obsolete.*
**Buckminster Fuller**

After a devastating terror attack in Christchurch, New Zealand, where fifty Muslims were gunned down as they prayed, the extraordinarily compassionate response of their Prime Minister, Jacinda Ardern, brought her to the front and center of the world stage.

She addressed the terrorist directly, just a few hours after the attack, telling him, "You may have chosen us, but we utterly reject and condemn you." She wore a black headscarf the following day, meeting with Muslim leaders and asking them what they would like her to do. She also refused to focus on Islamophobia as the root cause of the attack, instead looking at the deeper underlying causes of an incident of this nature. The whole world watched as she responded with compassion and heart.

During that time, there was one question repeated over and over again on global social media. "What if we all had leadership of this kind?" Many of us paused to reflect on what our world would be like if Ardern's approach had not been extraordinary, but rather a reflection of how most world leaders respond in such a moment as this. Humanity craves this kind of heart-centered leadership, and longs for a world where the decision makers have their hearts engaged with their minds. Many of us have also felt the sting of pessimism that we will never see such consistent global leadership in our lifetime. We have the sense that our system was not created so that such global leadership can thrive.

This predicament leaves two choices. The first is to try and "fix" the current predicament that has led to the election of the kinds of leaders who are motivated by personal power and greed. There are many individuals in activism and politics who are working to create solutions, and while we deeply value and support their efforts, we also recognize that an overhaul of this nature is likely going to take some time. The second choice is to create a system that immediately addresses these challenges.

To create a system in which a group of leaders are already centered on creating a fairer and more just society. What if such a group were suddenly given the wealth and power to make social changes that impact the good of all? If you can imagine such a system, *that's* what we've created with Artemes.

In this chapter we'll outline how the Aware Leadership System works, along with the thinking behind it, and in the next chapter we'll share

the economic aspect, so that you can see what happens with a system of leadership with economic power that shatters many of the existing paradigms. In this way we can make lasting change in this world with leadership we respect at the helm.

## WHY THE CURRENT SYSTEM ISN'T WORKING

History has consistently shown that leaders are often quickly corrupted. This is particularly true in corporate settings, where leadership is usually governed by profit margins and cost cutting. In the US, this mentality filters through our electoral system, so that large corporations fund all presidential candidates who then remain in the pockets of the corporations who paid for their position. Politicians who try to break from this system, are usually sidelined as a result. Thus, US political leaders are led in whatever directions the corporations that rule them decide. Revolutionary change cannot take place under a system such as this.

As Marianne Williamson outlines in *A Politics of Love*:

> *The main organizing principle of American society today is not democracy; it is short-term profit maximization of multinational corporations. Our government does not now function to protect citizens from overreach by corporations, so much as it works to protect corporations from all those pesky citizens who keep demanding that their rights be respected.*

She goes on to say:

> *Democracy is not the enemy of an amoral economic system; it's simply inconvenient to an amoral economic system. The thieves who stole our democracy—a thriving middle class, accessible health care, a robust education system, and proper environmental stewardship— didn't use brute force to knock down the door. No, they used the soft, insidious power of political propaganda that no seriously thinking person should have fallen for.*[1]

We can no longer let these systems of leadership steer the world's affairs. Instead, we need free and enlightened individuals to be at the helm. These leaders will move to the beat of a new drum with priorities based on the good of all rather than the survival of the individual. This type of leadership is what sets the Artemes System apart from all other governing bodies that have gone before.

## Feeling the Resonance

Great leadership is much more than something that is achieved through building empires and commanding global companies. A great leader—as far as the Artemes System is concerned—is someone who transmits the resonance of awareness. When you meet someone who is a self-realized, aware, and awake human being, you will likely feel uplifted. It is often said in spiritual circles that these beings produce higher energy waves, which interact with your being and naturally elevate your own frequency. You hear about this when people who meet the Dalai Lama or other enlightened beings report a change in perspective or feeling simply by being in their presence. This is

why we often feel at our best when we encounter such spiritual life mastery.

This occurs because certain emotions are said to run at a higher frequency than others. Love, compassion, and joy, for example, run at a higher resonance than anger, hate, apathy, and fear.

I asked an electrical engineering friend of mine to describe from a physics perspective what happens when a high-frequency person comes in contact with a low-frequency person. He shared that if the waves are similar enough to superimpose on each other, the result is a combination of constructive and destructive waves. This means that the higher frequency wave will be brought down to the lower frequency, and the lower frequency wave will increase in amplitude, until both express roughly the same.

Hypothetically, if two people share a room for an extended period of time—one experiencing a difficult and dark moment, and one experiencing an elevated moment—the higher frequency would boost the lower frequency and the lower frequency would reduce the higher. It's similar to putting a hot piece of metal in a bucket of water: the water will cool the metal and the metal will heat the water.

So basically, the high- and low-energy people would level one another out: something that you have likely experienced in person from time to time.

However, what about when a being such as the Dalai Lama enters a room full of thousands of other beings vibrating at a lower level than he is? It would seem that he is somehow emanating high-energy waves and insulating himself from the waves of others. This insulating property is likely a result of his enlightened state, in which he vibrates with the energy of the universe.

In addition to this, the ability to focus awareness and consciousness enables a higher energy being of this nature to remain in such a state. A being such as this can likely raise the consciousness of a room through intention and awareness.

Something similar can be found in critical communication cables, which are used in utilities, where shielded cable prevents the signal from being interfered with by external signals. Assuming someone in high resonance can "shield" themselves from the drain of low resonance, it is possible to remain at high resonance, no matter the external situation.

The degree of this effect depends on the depth of resilience that each person has. Going back to the analogy of water and metal, if you place a droplet of water on a large piece of hot metal, the metal doesn't really cool while the water is superheated, and vice versa: a hot bolt thrown into the ocean will have an imperceptible effect on the water temperature.

If we can develop a high frequency, based on compassion and love, while simultaneously insulating ourselves with awareness, we can naturally have an influence on those around us, bringing them up to a higher energy state.

This may be where the old saying "You are who you surround yourself with" comes from. Surround yourself with those who vibrate at a high level, and they will elevate your own energy. Surround yourself with friends who vibrate at a low level, and they will lower your energy.

I experienced this personally while riding in a minibus from San Agustinillo to the airport at Huatulco, Mexico—there was a man just in front of me whose energy I could feel strongly. He sat quietly, simply observing everything around him. The hour drive through the jungle, up and over ridges and down and through valleys of streams was normally fast and hectic. This trip was different. This passenger was somehow affecting me and everyone else on the bus, including the driver. The bus seemed to float across the landscape. Once we got to the airport, he got out and gave the driver one of the most heartfelt hugs I have ever seen. I went off to register at the front desk and once inside the terminal, I continued observing him, still affected by his energy. During the flight to Mexico City, I could still feel his presence.

When we landed, I finally approached him. "I was in the bus with you earlier, and we were on the plane from Huatulco. I don't want to assume anything, but I feel that you are different," I told him.

"Thank you. I think," he replied.

It turned out he'd been meditating for six months at Hridaya Yoga, a meditation retreat center in Mazunte. The effects of his practice were palpable. Yet unlike the Dalai Lama, he hadn't spent his whole life in spiritual practice of this kind. He was actually a farmer from upstate Washington.

This experience of being in the presence of an aware being, whether a random stranger who has spent six months in meditation, or a spiritual leader such as the Dalai Lama, naturally elevates us. Knowing this, what would happen if one hundred beings (who had previously been lost in thought and experiencing life at a lower energy level) suddenly awakened? What would happen if ten people on your street awakened? What if millions of individuals around the world began to awaken too?

It is likely that these higher energy beings will begin elevating lower energy beings into higher states. This is how Artemes will begin changing the world in a physical way. The universe will begin vibrating at a higher frequency, and every being on the planet will begin feeling the effects. This begins with the Council of the Aware.

## Introducing the Council of the Aware

Growth of the Artemes System will begin with a core of eleven high-frequency individuals. We plant these seeds of beings and let the awakening grow from there: from awakened individual to awakened individual. The first eleven select their own eleven, based upon what they experience an "awakened" individual to be. This is essential, as it is difficult to put into words, let alone define, what an awakened being is. This is why we start with the initial seeds of awakened beings. Each of these individuals is so highly developed that they can immediately see if someone is trapped in the societal paradigm (sleeping), or has broken free (awakened). These eleven individuals will then relay this knowledge to the next 121 selected into the system, then the 121 will select and relay this knowledge to the individuals that they select, and so on.

As a winner-loser economy is often what prevents individuals from having the ability to be creative and conscious, we will reward each level of growth with Artemes cryptocurrency (which we will outline in further detail in the next chapter). The initial eleven beings will be rewarded greatly, so that they can be free to focus on what is needed to support humanity in these times. Individuals selected at each successive stage will be awarded with ever-decreasing amounts of Artemes cryptocurrency.

We choose eleven individuals who are trustworthy and not centrally motivated by personal gain. We choose people from different faiths, who are open and respectful to the faiths of all. These individuals have created their own relationship with both science and spirituality. Each one has a notable focus on justice and equality in either the work that they do, or the way they show up in the world. These are heart-centered and compassionate beings who are intelligent, personable, and kind.

In creating this system, we are aware that not every one of the leaders chosen would be loved and revered by everyone in the Artemes System. If we can each put aside our personal preferences based on any past judgments, and look at the body of the leadership as a whole, then we can start to focus on the power that these leaders have to create change in the world around us.

Currently we have a system where 44.8 percent of the world's wealth is controlled by 1 percent of the people.[2] We know what happens when a system of this nature is founded on greed and personal gain, because we are living in the wake of that. We need to quickly and effectively move beyond this paradigm.

When we combine this leadership with the economic model we present in the chapter that follows this one, we give them the resources to tackle some of the challenges that we face collectively, such as closing socio-economic gaps, tackling issues around racial, sexual, and gender inequality, working with the refugee crisis, dealing with environmental issues, creating a fairer education system that is accessible to all, and ensuring everyone has access to a roof over their heads, with clean water and food for all. The Council of the Aware will not only raise awareness about these issues—they will have the financial resources to tackle them too. In many ways, this means that the eleven leaders become part of the consciousness and the soul of the world with the power to make change in all they do.

If that seems like a lot on the shoulders of eleven people, the Artemes System does not stop there. Each of those eleven leaders will choose eleven others, with only two requirements—each of these eleven must cover a specific specialty, and they must be awake. The leader who chooses the eleven will be the one who decides if their selected beings are awake. They choose people in their networks and circles that they know reflect similar values to the ones that Artemes holds. So now we have a network of eleven individuals with 121 people beneath them who are working towards the same goal, making advances in areas such as justice, governance, health, etc. These 132 individuals will work for the Council of the Aware. And again, each of those choose a further eleven, until the network of the Aware Leadership begins to take root and spread across the globe.

The international alliance of female elders—known as the Council of Indigenous Grandmothers—has already been doing this on a small

scale, and both the Iroquois Council and the councils in Athens, Greece were similar to this idea. What differs from these in the Artemes System is that we have created a way to financially bolster these individuals, so that they have financial power to make lasting change in the world.

## The Power to Create Change

The Aware Leadership, combined with the conscious cryptocurrency (which we will outline in the chapter that follows) is how we build an economy on mindfulness, awareness, and compassion rather than on profit alone. This means that Artemes will be able to redistribute wealth around the world. This new world consciousness is combined with the Artemes Training that we present in the third part of this book. This ensures that we create and foster a climate of trust and cooperation, because everyone who is involved is also either aware, or working towards waking up from the illusion of the current paradigm.

This is in contrast to the power that already exists in the world. If you think about corporations and much of the current world leadership, there is no incentive to help others because both groups are built on the winner-takes-all model where the only incentives come at the price of hurting others. Yet when we have leaders who are not attached to corporate gain, we can start creating changes, because the individuals involved will lose nothing from their own resources in order to create that change.

So far, we have run our planet as if it is a company—or more precisely, a few global companies have been running the planet as if it is their own—and now, the focus of how we run it will dramatically shift. It is the 99 percent of us who must stand up to correct this situation. It is unrealistic to expect those who are benefiting from it to correct it themselves.

When leadership operates from consciousness, it creates a tidal wave of change that affects all involved. Individuals who have been operating in survival, because their circumstances have created a sink-or-swim mentality, will be given the resources to thrive. It's been previously highlighted that many of the global issues we face are born out of an "us" and "them" mentality that comes from a survival mindset. Yet when we take individuals out of survival and give them the resources to know that they are safe, many of the issues they have been fighting against begin to fade away. When there is less survival and more awareness, peace begins to take root.

## In the Beginning

In the beginning stages of the development of the Artemes System, very little in the world will change. The initial eleven enlightened beings are already awakened. Their involvement will not raise the consciousness level of the planet as their spiritual energy is already very high. Similarly, it is likely that most of the beings introduced into the Artemes System in the next stages will already have high levels of awareness, and thus the world will appear unchanged at this point. It is later in its development that the Artemes System will begin to have an impact.

Stages of the Artemes System are as follows:

Stage 1 - 11 beings

Stage 2 - 121 beings

Stage 3 - 1,331 beings

Stage 4 - 161,051 beings

Stage 5 - 1,771,561 beings

Stage 6 - 19,487,171 beings

Stage 7 - 214,358,881 beings

Stage 8 - 2,357,948,000 beings

It is during Stage 5 of development that the world will begin to change. Those individuals from Stage 4 (161,051 awakened beings) will each select their eleven awakened individuals. Some of the individuals selected at this stage may know eleven awakened individuals, but many will likely not. It is at this point—the Artemic Tipping Point— that the system shifts from aggregating already-awakened individuals to actually awakening beings.

The Artemic Tipping Point signifies the moment in time that the world will begin to change. From this point forward, many asleep (low vibrational energy) individuals will be awakened (into high vibrational energy beings). Suddenly, those of us who have been lost in regrets of the past or hopes for the future begin to get a solid footing in the here and now. Instead of existing in fear, anger, joylessness, apathy, and confusion (all lower frequency emotions), we will collectively begin experiencing more joy, happiness, and compassion (all higher frequency emotions). As more and more individuals are awakened, the vibrational frequency that surrounds us all will begin to rise. This will slowly but surely impact the whole world around us.

Stage 4 individuals will be searching for people who still might be asleep, but where consciousness is close to the surface. Many of us know people like this—those who are introspective, sensitive, and thoughtful, but are still reactive to the world around them. They have not yet started their search, but could easily be jolted into action. These individuals will be the true beginning of the conscious revolution.

After Stage 5 is complete, nearly 2 million people will participate in the Artemes System. Many of these will be newly awakened individuals operating at a high energy frequency for the first time. It may be hard to put your finger on it, but things will begin to feel different from this point. There will be a different vibe as more and more beings begin resetting to higher energy states. There will be more joy and happiness on social media. Encounters at the grocery store will be more pleasant. The atmosphere at the office will be a little more open. Overall, there will be an air of greater potential for humanity. At this stage of development, the conscious revolution will have become palpable.

By this time, Artemes will be known worldwide. Those who are still asleep will have heard of it and likely know someone who is awakened and is now part of the conscious revolution. Social media, podcasts, blogs, and vlogs will be buzzing with the high energy waves of the mass awakening. Oprah will be interviewing one of the initial eleven enlightened leaders to inquire what the conscious revolution will mean for us all. Everyone not in Artemes will be wondering what it means to awaken. In essence, the world will be preparing the next level of awakenings.

Those still outside the system will be Google-searching "How do you awaken?" Fortunately for them, the answers will be out there, as there will be millions of awakened beings in the world vibrating at the high-frequency aware state. This energy will be felt by every organism in the world (person, animal, and plant) and will be the antidote to the social climate that we are experiencing today.

After Stage 6 of outward growth, there will be over 20 million awakened individuals from every corner of the globe. These individuals will then become the leaders as they select and awaken their eleven beings. By this point the world has become a new place. The global energy will have risen to such a high level that all aspects of life will be touched by this new energy of consciousness. Those outside of the system, who have been feeling the ripples of the global shift, will be engulfed by a tidal wave of consciousness.

Even if you want to hold onto the old societal paradigm, at this point, it will be impossible. The energy frequency of the world will have changed and it will be impossible not to be naturally pulled up by the higher energy levels that surround you. Therefore, it will not only be the individual from Stage 6 that is awakening you—it will be the millions of high energy individuals that surround you who are doing it at the same time.

After Stage 7, Artemes will include nearly 250 million awakening individuals. At this point others will have total trust in the system (through all the media exposure and the general truth of the system) and will want to get into it. They will naturally step on their own path of awakening. This will intensify as the wave grows larger and larger.

When we all begin vibrating at these higher levels, it will induce a state of bliss within each of us. At this point in the development, asleep beings will have to do very little to awaken, as the vibrational energy around them will naturally elevate them to this state.

After Stage 8, there will be over 2.5 billion people in the Artemes System. The world, by then, will be a new place. If you imagine billions in the world buzzing at a blissfully high energy, you can also likely imagine how this would have the potential to stamp out fear and apathy. The energy set point of the world would change.

## A New Vision

It is at this point that a new vision for the world will emerge. From our current state of consciousness we are unable to push too strongly for a new vision, as this new vision would be created from within our current low energy paradigm (which is why we have had many failed attempts to change the system in the past). As J. Krishnamurti suggested, changing one system to another (capitalism to communism, for instance) from within our current state of mind is the equivalent of changing the curtains inside our prison cell. Things may look a little different, but we're still imprisoned.

Once the egosphere has been drained and the sea of consciousness has risen, humanity will then be ready to create the new systems that will govern us. Here, we will begin to make rules and systems from the perspective of compassion and care, instead of the competition and fear which our present system is based upon. Issues that used to frighten us (climate change, inequality, hunger) will be

acknowledged and corrected.

This time of creation will not be forced like a square peg into a round hole. This is because the Council of the Aware will be at the helm of humanity's ship. These most enlightened beings will steer us into a future that will naturally take form. This piloting will not have to be heavy-handed, as is the case with most of today's leaders, but will only require a light touch to stay the course.

As their birthright, each human should have food, clean water, shelter, and healthcare. As one, we will create systems that will make these rights commonplace for every being on this planet. As a species, we will have evolved to a place where this is now possible. Within the higher vibrational energy of awareness, this truth will begin to take form.

Wise and awakened political theorists and economists (chosen and directed by the Council of the Aware) will create something that is fresh and new and that will provide for all beings everything they need to prosper. This will not be socialism, communism, or capitalism; but it may contain the best elements of all these systems.

## Some General Rules of the Artemes System

An odd number (11) was chosen as a beginning number for purposes of voting. The Council of the Aware will be voting on how to appropriately begin dealing with world issues, such as hunger, inequality, the Amazon burning, coral reefs diminishing, education, insect populations plummeting, climate change, diminishing fish stock, dirty water, plastic oceans, etc. There will be a variety of ways to address them, and a clear path to action will be needed. The odd number of voters will make this more easily achievable.

For the initial enlightened eleven beings, two individuals each will be selected from each populated continent in the world, the only exception being Oceania (Australia, New Guinea, New Zealand and other smaller countries), which—owing to its smaller population—will receive one position.

A majority of the first eleven individuals selected (at least six out of the initial eleven) will be women. Women's brains are wired differently than men's[3] and it appears that women show more compassion and less ego than their male counterparts. Also, men have controlled the power for millennia and this testosterone-fueled era has produced much of the war and other detrimental systems that now govern humanity. For our new start, it's time to move towards a more heart-centered leadership. Similarly, a majority of those selected in the initial eleven will be people of color.

## SUMMING UP

History has consistently shown that leaders in the current paradigm are often quickly corrupted. In the corporate settings, leadership is usually governed by profit margins and cost cutting. We can no longer let these systems of leadership pilot the world's affairs.

### In Artemes we are:

- Building a system which starts with eleven high-frequency individuals. They are trustworthy and not centrally motivated by personal gain.

- Inviting them to select eleven individuals beneath them. Each of these eleven must cover a specific specialty, such as justice, governance and health, and they must be awake.

- Operating from conscious leadership, which creates a tidal wave of change that affects all involved.

- Creating, as the system grows, an Artemic Tipping point—a significant moment in the world where things begin to change.

Now that we have outlined the Council of the Aware, in the next chapter we will look at a new economic system that will disrupt the current paradigm.

# CHAPTER FIVE
## CONSCIOUS CRYPTOCURRENCY

*Profit is important only as a necessary condition, not as the ultimate goal.*
**Muhammad Yunus**

Most of the challenges with our economic systems exist in a context of ultimate capitalism which always results in some form of exploitation. Many visionaries have echoed that humanity has the potential to evolve beyond the winners-and-losers paradigm into a system that is fairer for all. However, our current system contains so many elements of socially acceptable slavery. Those who benefit from the spoils of this system are so entrenched in their benefits and rewards, that instead of trying to dismantle the system, Artemes has created one that is built on the values of unity and love in this world. So equality, compassion—all the values that we hold dear—become the driving force of the cryptocurrency, enabling the wealth it generates to contribute to greatness in the world.

Joseph Stiglitz, the expert in economics we mentioned earlier, has taken a stand against cryptocurrencies for a very good reason. In 2017 he shared that one of the biggest problems with cryptocurrencies is that they don't serve any socially useful function.[1] With Artemes, we turn this challenge around, creating a cryptocurrency system that is *built* on social purpose.

In this chapter we'll introduce the unique Artemes cryptocurrency system that creates an alternative to the current system of power and greed. We'll share why this system is needed on an economic level, and how it can disrupt the current system, closing socio-economic gaps and creating a sustainable economy for all involved. As Nobel Peace Prize winner Muhammad Yunus asked in his book *Building Social Business,* "Is there a way that technology could serve human needs that is currently *not* being practiced?" Yunus called for "Adopting technology used by the wealthy to the needs of the poor,"[2] and that is what we are doing at Artemes.

## Introducing Artemes Cryptocurrency

One of the biggest issues when trying to do economic social good is that the impact is often very limited and local. We tend to focus on the economic challenges of our own countries, without giving too much thought to the global economy. As Branko Milanovic points out in *Global Inequality,* "People in rich countries and their governments are very concerned with providing (at least legally) equal treatment to all people living within the country's borders. At the same time, they are largely indifferent to workers outside their borders."[3]

The other issue is that we often try to do good within the system that created the problems in the first place, and end up with a disconnect from the needs of the people who we want to help. As Anand Giridharadas highlights in *Winners Take All: The Elite Charade of Changing the World,* "Often when people set out to do the thing they are already doing and love to do and know how to do, and they promise grand civilization benefits as a spillover effect, the solution is oriented around the solver's needs more than the world's—the win-wins, purporting to be about others, are really about you."[4]

We took both these understandings into careful consideration when building the new cryptocurrency that we have called Artemes. There are many cryptocurrencies out there, which people from all walks of life buy—from first-time investors to seasoned billionaires—hoping that they pick up a short-term profit. The most successful example of this is Bitcoin, which started at close to zero and, at its peak, each coin was valued at $19,783.[5]

Although Bitcoin sparked a whole host of similar coins, only a very small portion of them have, so far, escalated in value. Most of them start from being valued at close to nothing and don't grow very much from there.

Artemes differs from these systems in that it puts a cause and a meaning in the system. Like all cryptocurrencies, it is going to create profits, but it is also designed for good. This is a win-win for all, and is what Matthew Bishop and Michael Green termed philanthropic capitalism, in their 2008 book *Philanthropic Capitalism, How the Rich Can Save the World.*[6]

# HOW ARTEMES BECOMES VALUABLE

There are four separate elements that enable Artemes cryptocurrency to become valuable. They are:

## 1 - The Supply is Limited

One of the elements of Artemes that will make it fairer for all relates to how we have created a system of supply and demand. If you ask the average person what the most valuable commodity on earth is, they would likely say gold. But there was a time when salt was the most valuable commodity on earth. In fact, the word "salary" originates from salt.[7] And a phrase that is still used today, "Not worth his salt," stems from the practice of trading slaves for salt in ancient Greece.[8] It was only when we realized that the sea was full of salt that it became a much less precious commodity.

In unconscious capitalistic scenarios, supply and demand has been used to the detriment of the users. For example, Jordan sneakers were made in a system of scarcity so that the top ten most expensive ones ever sold range from $10,000 for a pair of Air Jordan V, to $104,000 for Air Jordan 12 (Flu Game).[9] Although this is a modern example of supply and demand, we've been operating under similar systems for some time.

These unfair systems of supply and demand are also misused in times of disaster. When Hurricane Maria hit Puerto Rico in 2017, there were limited flights that could bring the people to the USA. Flights from Puerto Rico to New York are usually a couple of hundred dollars. At that time they went up to almost $10,000. This is another example of ultimate capitalism that exploits those who are part of the system. We quote Göran Therborn once again from *The Killing Fields of Inequality*,

"Exploitation is universally regarded as the worst form of inequality."[10]

One of the challenges with limited supply is that the people that have access to the coins first have flexibility of knowledge. They get unfair access and a bigger pot, just because they had information on availability early on. However, with Artemes we have not only contradicted the notion that you need scarcity for valuation—we have created a staged release plan so that we can benefit a mass amount of people.

As we highlighted in the chapter before this one, each of the eleven members of the Council of the Aware chooses eleven people, who in turn choose eleven people, and so on. This creates a number of different stages in Artemes, which relates to the value of the coins. Below you will see the table that relates to the staged release process.

| Category | Total Individuals | Share of Ownership(%) |
| --- | --- | --- |
| Aware Leaders | 11 | < 0.001% |
| Next 11 | 121 | < 0.01% |
| Next 11 | 1,331 | < 0.05% |
| Next 11 | 14,641 | < 0.1% |
| Next 11 | 161,051 | < 0.5% |
| Next 11 | 1,771,561 | < 2% |
| Next 11 | 19,487,171 | < 7% |
| Next 11 | 214,358,881 | < 15% |
| Next 11 | 2,357,948,000 | < 50% |
| Total | 2,593,742,768 | ~75% |

Outside of the staged release plan, we have very detailed rules on limitation of investment, sales options, etc., to keep the scarcity element of valuation going. (You can read all the details of the economic model and its implementation details at www.artemes.global)

## 2 - Trust

Most other cryptocurrency systems are built on greed; Artemes stands apart from them because it is philanthropic, and also transparent. It is based on trust.

To understand how this trust is generated, we need to take a step back and look at the context in which the usual systems of economy are mapped in our social conditioning. We need to go back to the source to understand the principles of economic strategy, and one way to explore this is through game theory.

Game theory is the study of strategic decision-making, and its core pioneers were mathematicians John von Neumann and John Nash, and economist Oskar Morgenstern. It is largely used in Behavioral Economics, but we practice game theory a lot in our daily lives without even realizing we are doing so. While we are weighing up the odds of any situation, or working out strategies for a move we intend to make, we are practicing game theory.

One of the most common examples of game theory is explained by the prisoner's dilemma. Imagine two people who have just been arrested for a crime that they jointly committed. You've probably seen this scene in countless movies and TV shows. The one where the FBI agent tells the suspect, "Your partner has confessed. If you confess too it reduces your sentence." You enter into that game without really knowing if your partner has confessed or not. If you both confess, you will likely both go to jail for a medium amount of time. If you say you are not guilty and your partner confesses, he goes to jail for a long time. If both of you remain silent and say nothing, there will be yet another outcome in the game. So you weigh up the odds without really knowing the true components of the game, and in such a scenario, there is more likely going to be a winner and a loser. This is why the prisoner's dilemma is often described as "a situation where individual decision-makers always have an incentive to choose in a way that creates a less than optimal outcome for the individuals in the group."[11]

The prisoner's dilemma is also used to describe dilemmas in economy, where the same winner-loser paradigm has been the driving force behind much of our economic decision-making. It is used to model competitive behaviors between economic agents and it helps to predict when certain firms are going to operate in price-fixing or collusion.

Within game theory, we also have the possibility of Nash equilibrium. This is where the players of the game operate in a way that is least harmful to the other players. You see this in stock markets when the price of a share has a temporary drop and the shareholders don't immediately sell their stock because they are operating with an understanding that if they instantly pull out of every deal when the market shifts slightly, there would ultimately be no stock market. So they learn to play in ways that create more equilibrium within the system.

The difference between the prisoner's dilemma and Nash equilibrium is that the first supposes that both sides are kept in the dark (and are thus combatants), while the second supposes that both sides are aware of the potential outcomes (and thus are teammates). With Artemes, we are looking to create an economic Nash equilibrium in which all

sides are aware and making the best decisions for the most people.

How all this relates to our conscious cryptocurrency is that systems of game theory that create the prisoner's dilemmas are ones where the game is not being played fairly. In contrast, we decided to create a system that is built on equilibrium and trust. Imagine a cryptocurrency system that was fully transparent. One where no information about the game was being hidden from others. That's what we have created with Artemes.

## How the Council of the Aware Builds Trust

Even though the basic foundation of cryptocurrency systems is built on the fact that they can't be rigged, *many cryptocurrency systems have still been susceptible to rigging and unfair play.* This is because the average cryptocurrency system is set up by individuals who stand to gain personal benefit, within the system of "winner takes all," which we have been entrained to operate in. This issue is highlighted in *An Intro to Cryptoeconomics* by Vitalik Buterin.[12] [13]

Buterin shows that the only way that cryptocurrency can fairly work is when there is a minority group that everyone trusts. This is known as zero-proof knowledge which is one of the main components of cryptocurrency systems that ensure they are built on trust and fairness. What we've created with Artemes ensures we have this system in place, because the eleven leaders in the Council of the Aware are selected precisely so that trust becomes an integral part of this system. You may not resonate with every leader in the council. But what we have created is the closest to trust that a system such as this can get. When we put incredible leaders with exceptional intentions at the center of the framework of the system, we create one that has humanistic motivations at its heart.

We put the eleven world leaders at the center and they are given their coins, because the more value their coins have, the more good they can do in the world. These are the most powerful people in the system, not because they have bought their way there, but because of the good they have already done in the world. They choose eleven people beneath them who they trust, and so the system continues.

The reason we won't open Artemes up for sale immediately is that it would just be like any other system where the already wealthy could corner the market. We ensure, through the system that we create, that we have a fair game for all. (Visit our site for the specifics at www.artemes.global)

### 3 - Tradability and the Market
Earlier in this chapter we gave the example of how salt was once a highly valuable commodity. Similarly, right now, gold is extremely valuable because it is scarce, and it can be traded for money globally. In the same way, Artemes cryptocurrency will be able to be traded with all other cryptocurrency and real currency around the world. (We have some minimal restrictions which you can read about at www.artemes.global)

### 4 - People Prefer to Act for Good When They Have the Option
If people have the option to make only profit, or make the profit plus do good, they will choose the latter. That is one of the main reasons that Artemes will gain value fast. A large number of cryptocurrency

investors will be interested in purchasing a currency that is not only high in economic profit for them, but can also make them feel part of a bigger cause and community. This sense of community has been seen in past coins, such as Dogecoin, where an internet meme for dogs sparked a coin community that—at its peak in 2014—was valued at $60 million. In addition, many successful billionaires, such as Elon Musk, Bill Gates, and Michael Bloomberg, are known to carry out philanthropic investment. This means that Artemes has a higher potential success rate because philanthropic investors will be drawn to taking part, and Artemes can be a bridge between their philanthropic work and their investments.

## HOW ARTEMES SUPPORTS THE ECONOMICALLY CHALLENGED

There are two different ways that Artemes closes socio-economic gaps.

### A - Dividend Awarded to Those Within the System

Gradually, as Artemes starts to become valuable, it is going to have a Universal Basic Income (UBI) style dividend created within it. This means that all participants will be given a stipend.

If you buy a stock in a company such as Amazon, every year that company gives a certain small amount of money to everyone who owns the stocks of that company. Artemes will have a similar aim, so we are profit sharing en masse, so that part of the wealth is given back to the people who have the shares.

## B - Wealth Generation Given to Good Causes

In his book *Building Social Businesses,* Muhammad Yunus asks, "How can vital goods (financial services, healthcare) be made available at the same level of quality for poor people in the developing world as for wealthy people in the developed nations?"[14] Artemes aims to address this question with its outcomes. From all of the wealth that is generated, there will be an internal income tax, and a part of that is saved for good causes, which are selected by the Council of the Aware. Taxes will be used to ensure that the Council of the Aware always has the funds available to create the change in the world that is needed. These include causes in areas such as:

- Justice
- Infrastructure
- Arts
- Governance
- Environment
- Economics
- Health
- Relations and Media
- Science
- Spirituality
- Education

This will ensure that Artemes is led by its philanthropic agenda (unlike many modern, capitalist companies which tack on philanthropy as an afterthought).

## The Negative Impact of Cryptocurrency

Although much of this chapter has outlined the positive impact that cryptocurrency can have, we also want to acknowledge its shortcomings. One of the core aims of Artemes is to contribute to environmental reform, yet one of the criticisms of cryptocurrency is that it is very bad for the environment. It consumes a significant amount of energy, because it runs on computers. The percentage of power in the world that is dedicated to Bitcoin alone—due to its mining centers—is the equivalent of the power used by New Zealand in a year.[15] Although there is not an ideal solution to this in today's paradigm, Artemes is offsetting its own carbon footprint by making sure that the percentage of profits used in the environmental sector is *greater* than the other sectors.

## SUMMING UP

Most of the challenges with our current economic systems are encountered in a context of ultimate capitalism which always results in some form of exploitation. In contrast, we are introducing a new cryptocurrency which we have called Artemes, which is designed to disrupt the current economic system. Artemes differs from common cryptocurrencies (which are motivated purely by profit), because it puts a cause and a meaning in the system, and is designed to do good in the world.

### ARTEMES BECOMES VALUABLE BECAUSE:

1. **The Supply is Limited** - Our system includes a staged release plan and rules on limitation of investment.
2. **There is Trust** - While the basic foundation of most cryptocurrency systems is built on greed, this system is philanthropic, and also transparent.
3. **It is Tradable and Marketable** - Artemes will be able to be traded with all other cryptocurrency and real currency around the world.
4. **People Prefer to Act for Good When They Have the Option** - For investors, Artemes will not only offer economic profit, but it can also make them feel part of a bigger cause and community.

## ARTEMES SUPPORTS THE ECONOMICALLY CHALLENGED BECAUSE:

A. **Dividends are Awarded to Those Within the System** - Profit is shared en masse, so that part of the wealth is given back to the people who have the shares.

B. **Wealth Generation is Given to Good Causes** - From all of the wealth that is generated, there will be an internal income tax, and a part of that is saved for good causes which are selected by the Council of the Aware.

Now that we have outlined the new Artemes cryptocurrency that will challenge the current economic paradigm, we'll move to Part Three of the book—The Artemes Training—which will enable you to go more deeply into your own personal awakening, so you can contribute to social growth with more awareness.

# ARTEMES
A Conscious Economic System for Creating
Equality in an Unbalanced World

PART THREE **3**

# ARTEMES
# TRAINING

The Artemes Training is the step-by-step approach that accompanies the development of aware leadership and the use of conscious cryptocurrency; it supports each Artemes community member to reach a state of awareness.

Few of us were ever given the tools to appropriately deal with this crazy ride. In Part Three of this book you'll find the basic concepts and practices that will enable you to have enough training to begin or continue your awakening.

This section is about awareness and awakening, and although there are many other books that cover this subject, what makes Artemes different is that your awakening will be directly tied into the Artemes System, so that you can receive currency in terms of Artemes coins.

In Part Two of this book we already highlighted how this system works and is designed to grow quickly with the participation in it. In this section we bring that system to life for you, so your personal growth is linked to the system as a whole.

# CHAPTER SIX
## Developing Awareness

> 99 *The individual has always had to struggle to keep from being overwhelmed by the tribe. To be your own [person] is hard business. If you try it, you will be lonely often, and sometimes frightened. But no price is too high to pay for the privilege of owning yourself.*
> **Rudyard Kipling**

The first step in the Artemes journey is opening to awareness. Many traditional spiritual paths have awareness as a central focus. The majority of those paths place individual awareness as the main goal of the practice so that we can wake up to the automatic programs and learned behaviors that have been running our lives so far.

In his book *The Conscious Mind*,[1] David Chalmers shares an imaginary world, consisting of zombie-like creatures. The zombies that exist in his world are identical to us, but lack the experience of consciousness

altogether. These zombies are functionally and psychologically the same as us, in that they process and react to similar stimuli, and play roles similar to ours, but the difference is that for them "all is dark inside." In other words, their prefrontal cortex—the conscious component of their brain—is not activated as it is in us.

Although most of us have access to the higher centers of our brain, they are not consistently activated in many of us. This means that, like the zombies in Chalmers' world, a great number of us exist without being in touch with our consciousness. We are going through the motions and reacting to stimuli in a pre-programmed way. We must each take individual responsibility to awaken from this zombie-like existence.

We all need to understand what we're waking up from, and that is a continuous loop of a zombie-like apocalypse that plays in our minds, and is barely connected to reality. It consists of memories of the past and dreams of the future, and is bolstered by many false teachings that we have learned along the way that are shared by other people who were lost in their own movies too. Waking up simply means that you understand that this is a dream and then you turn your awareness to the only thing that is real, which is: Being here and now. And from there, you notice all the distractions, the teachings, and the programs that pull you back into the past, or forward into the future, and you consistently and dynamically adjust until the dream no longer has the same power over you.

Individual awareness is a central part of the Artemes Training, but in addition, we are also focused on the awakening of humanity as a whole. Much of our work with awareness at Artemes also includes waking up to the way we human beings operate in our society. So we'll be looking at your individual awakening but also where it fits into our mass awakening. We'll be asking where you are asleep in your individual life, but also where we are collectively asleep in our cultures and in our societies, so that together we can contribute to a world that is fairer for all.

## Opening to Awareness

Early in life, awareness is more of a natural state for us. When I was young, I'd head into the woods and stay there all day. Looking back now, I see that as a child, I enjoyed the woods. Being there brought me closer to the feeling of oneness and of awareness that we don't articulate as children, but automatically know.

Most of us have lost touch with that child-like awareness that felt so natural to us back then. Therefore, the first step on your Artemes journey comes from your commitment to being aware. Part of that decision lies in the understanding that most of us don't want to be aware in all aspects of our lives.

Particularly if life is going well, or even if you are just scraping by, you probably tell yourself that everything is fine. Life has its issues and turmoils but overall, you're good. You tell yourself this because it keeps you pressing along through life. But maybe there is another part of you that feels like it's going through the motions. Living mechanically. Ticking the boxes. Jumping through the hoops. A nagging feeling that a part of you is slowly dying inside.

The truth is, if you want to awaken, you can't face that hurdle with the same mechanical approach that you've likely used for other things. It's not something to put on your vision board. It's not "10 steps and it's done." Yes, there are tools and practices that I will share in the pages that follow, but if you approach it like a fitness regime, you're going to fall short of really shaking yourself awake. You'll find another routine, another strategy, and instead of taking the layers off, you'll put another layer on. You'll find a new belief system to replace your old one. You might drop some habits or behaviors, but you will replace them with a new structure that is just more of the same. What we are suggesting here is a different approach.

In his book *Awareness*, spiritual teacher Anthony de Mello highlights how what most of us want is "relief," and not "cure." He shares a comical story:

> *Last year on Spanish television I heard a story about this gentleman who knocks on his son's door. "Jaime," he says, "wake up!" Jaime answers, "I don't want to get up, Papa."*
>
> *The father shouts, "Get up, you have to go to school." Jaime says, "I don't want to go to school." "Why not?" asks the father. "Three reasons," says Jaime. "First, because it's so dull; second, the kids tease me; and third, I hate school." And the father says, "Well, I am going to give you three reasons why you must go to school. First, because it is your duty; second, because you are forty-five years old, and third, because you are the headmaster." Wake up! Wake up! You've grown up. You're too big to be asleep. Wake up! Stop playing with your toys.[2]*

Most of us can relate to the headmaster. And even though this quote originated from the 1980s, it echoes through time. We don't want to let go of the things that give us comfort and relief. As de Mello goes on to share:

> *Most people tell you they want to get out of kindergarten, but don't believe them. Don't believe them! All they want you to do is to mend their broken toys. 'Give me back my wife. Give me back my job. Give me back my money. Give me back my reputation, my success.' This is what they want; they want their toys replaced. That's all. Even the best psychologist will tell you that—that people don't really want to be cured. What they want is relief; a cure is painful.[3]*

In short, if you are resistant to the process, it won't work. You have to put in consistent effort to wake up.

## Blocking Individual Awareness

On an individual level, many of us choose to ignore or turn our awareness away from the habits, the issues and the challenges that keep us locked in our individual identities. We tell ourselves, and the world, "This is just the way I am," and we attach to that which prevents us from growing because of the comfort we gain from it. Our relationship with these elements of ourselves is usually vastly complicated. For example, if we drink excessively—as I used to do—it's often not just the physical draw of alcohol that keeps us locked in that pattern. For me, it was also the social element that drinking would bring in. It was hard to turn down an all-night hot tub and dance party, even when they were happening most nights. In addition, if I look at my previous drinking

habits through the eyes of what I know now, it was also that there were deeply unrecognized parts of myself—deep in a hole in my soul that I was drinking to block out. Checking out and remaining in a haze with a curtain pulled down around me was comfortable. Only when I shined the light of awareness on what was really going on could I break down the layers and see my behavior for what it was.

Similarly, there is the person who cheats on their partner or has an affair, and I've been there too. If you want to operate in that reality without awareness, you can fool yourself that you are just living in the moment, free from the shackles of society, and following your truth, but the opposite is actually true. The only way I was able to have an affair was because I was shutting certain parts of myself out, blocking my awareness, switching off so I didn't need to look at myself.

These are just two of the ways that I blocked awareness in my own life and I share this with you, not from a place of guilt or shame, but from a place of peace where I have fully owned, and taken responsibility for, my behavior; I carefully studied the pathways in my brain that were leading me to justify the way I was showing up.

You don't need to be going on a drinking binge or having an affair to be blocking out your awareness. There are countless areas in our life where we fall asleep at the wheel, and justify the things we do as being socially acceptable, so therefore OK. We get home from work and we watch the TV for the whole evening, or binge-watch a show on Netflix. We can feel it sucking our soul out and sometimes there is a voice in us that questions it, but we push it away. We work double shifts because we have some kind of goal, such as going to college, moving to a different place, or seeing the world, but then we check out for a minute and suddenly we've spent all our money on clothes, jewelry or technology and we continue in that same loop where nothing seems to change. We set out with good intentions to eat well or exercise so that we can improve our health, and before we know it we are sitting in front of the TV with a bucket from KFC, wondering where it all fell down.

The truth is, our society is set up so that we continuously fall asleep. Our world is structured so that we check out, treat ourselves, buy things and do things that take us out of being present to this moment. And the first step on the Artemes ladder is accepting this, seeing it for what it is, and choosing a different way. In all honesty, that choice is probably one of the most challenging ones you will make. At first, you'll likely read these words, you'll see yourself in them, they'll probably make sense, and you'll make a commitment to being aware until an opportunity to check out comes along. Then you'll hear yourself say, "F*ck it," and you'll be back where you started. There's a chance that you'll go around on that merry-go-round, wrestling with yourself for months or years on end. Ask any addict who has tried to give up smoking or drinking for a while and they will tell you that this is the case. But there is another way. It requires much more than a half-assed commitment from you. It requires your willingness to open up to awareness from the very first moment of this program. To do that, you need a number of components in place. It requires you to be:

## 1 - Brutally honest with yourself
This includes owning everything that you know deep down is holding you back from being 100 percent here in this moment right

now. All the different ways you've ignored the feelings and voices that tell you that you are not being true, all the ways you've pushed down and squashed a feeling that you could do things a different way, all the ways you've bought into your social conditioning about your behaviors being OK. All of these need to be challenged in the face of awareness.

## 2 - Willing to face where you are asleep at the wheel

If there are a ton of these, you are probably going to want to break them down and tackle them one at a time, but fundamentally, if there is anywhere you decide "I know that it's destructive, but I'm going to keep it anyway," you are doing yourself a great disservice. The truth is, if you see it, if you shine your awareness on it and you know it is destructive, it's going to keep coming back again and again until you look it in the face. Once you are aware of it, there is no hiding from it, and you can either wrestle with it for the rest of your time on this earth or decide that you are going to bring awareness to it and change it. The key is that awareness on its own is a very crucial step, but it means little if you are going to continue going around in the same circles for eternity.

## 3 - Aware of the conflicting thoughts or emotions

There are probably going to be a bunch of conflicting voices or feelings that will try and convince you that your behavior is OK. So, as you are reading this now, there is likely some kind of recognition of the parts that you have been hiding from. I'm speaking directly to those parts with compassion and understanding (because I've been checked out in certain areas of my life and I know how it feels) and those parts of you are feeling heard and understood. The challenge is that there are going to be moments when you are not holding this book, when I'm not there with you, and when the old patterns kick in. The neurons of your brain have fired together so frequently when you've performed that habit or behavior in the past that as they start firing together again they are going to feel familiar. From that place you will likely hear a thought that tries to override your desire to change. That voice will send you right back to sleep if you let it, so part of your Artemes Training is going to be to prepare for it, to recognize it, to know what form it comes in and to remain aware even when it shows up. If you've ever seen a movie where the character has been brainwashed and they hear a certain word or phrase and they are hypnotized into suddenly being a terrorist or an assassin, this is what's happening in your brain in a moment like this, but in a much subtler way. You get the trigger from your external reality through your senses in the form of a word or phrase, an image or visual stimulus, a smell, or something you touch, and then you are swept away. It might not come as a voice. It might come more as a feeling with no words. What you are learning with the Artemes Training is to identify these responses and instead of becoming a zombie, marching to the tune of the stimuli, you develop tools and strategies to wake yourself up right away.

So what we've identified here is that both your thoughts and your feelings can hijack you in these moments and lead you to falling back to sleep. In the two chapters that follow, we're going to hit you with a number of strategies for the mind and the emotions so that you can shake yourself awake in the moments when you've gone back to sleep.

**WHERE ARE YOU:** Do you think you're asleep? Most of us would answer no to this question. Most of us don't think that we are. Are you willing to consider that at least a part of you is in a lifetime trance? If you can be truly fine with the possibility that you might just be living a waking dream, then we can start from there.

Part of the draw of Artemes is that it is created so that there is an incentive to awaken. We deliberately built the cryptocurrency system because it creates a force that will pull you in the direction of awakening. Some more conventional spiritual teachers would say that finance and spirituality should not mix. Yet in this modern world, bringing both together enables us to incentivize the process further, bringing along those who might otherwise not be interested, and in the process, creating an aware economic class to lead humanity forward. And in that space, we create the potential for each individual who participates to crack their shell.

## 4 - Aware of the Roles that You Play

Part of your opening to awareness is coming to terms with the roles that you play for others. These include cultural roles and personal roles.

If you've ever visited another country, one of the first things you likely noticed is the contrast between the socio-cultural roles of that culture and your own. Traveling opens our eyes because we get to see a reflection of what we thought were social norms, but were actually learned behaviors.

When first traveling to places outside of America, such as Mexico and Spain, I was surprised to see the degree of physical contact between same sexes. Not in a sexual way at all, but people were just much more free with their kisses and contact in general. It was definitely a beautiful eye-opener for me. Each culture has often silently created rules for our behavior that we adopt as if they were true. When you step outside of your culture, you are forced to face the fact that what you thought was 'normality' was actually something you were trained to do. Each of us, as we become more aware, needs to be open to questioning our social conditioning. I'm assuming that one of the reasons you are reading this book is that you know that many of our cultures have lost their way socially. Many of the practices and norms that are still socially acceptable are part of the reason that some very smart people are saying that we are threatening our very survival on this planet. Whatever the reality around this viewpoint, each of us needs to own the different elements of our social conditioning that are contributing to this collective disruption, so we can face them and change them, one by one. This is one of the guiding principles of Artemes.

## Individual Roles

Breaking down roles includes looking at all the things you believe you are, and realizing that they don't make up your essence. You learn to see past your name, your job, and any other label society imprinted you with, so that you can experience your truth beyond the layers that were imposed upon you.

As individuals in this society, we are told by our teachers, parents,

preachers, friends, or enemies who or what we are. This starts with a name that is stamped upon us at birth, and continues with a constant narrative, which creates for each of us the perception of ourselves that is built upon what others have told us. These untruths create layers that obscure your true self.

> **QUESTION EVERYTHING:** Questioning everything is the key to reaching this place. Especially question all that you absolutely believe to be true. If you were born in the US, is your essence truly American, or is that just a label that you have come to identify with? If you'd been born five miles over the border in Canada, would that have changed who you are? Can you see yourself beyond the label of your nationality? Question your career. Really examine the identities that have come with the role you were either assigned or you chose.

Roles are linked to survival (something we'll explore in greater depth in chapter 8 on navigating emotions). Many of us wrongly believe that our personal traits are a choice; however, when we pull back the curtain that has been concealing our awareness, what we start to see is that we learned to play roles that kept us safe. From a tribal point of view, we are wired to fit in because this is essential to our survival. As we grow up, we get approval or disapproval from those around us about certain behaviors and we learn to play roles that please others so that we can survive to fit in. Then when we get to adulthood, what we think is our personality is often only a collection of roles that we have not seen were shaped by the feedback of others—roles that we assume to be the real us. We keep on playing these roles until our awareness emerges and we shake ourselves awake, carefully assessing the difference between what is true to us and what we assumed to be true.

## AWARE OF BEING AWARE

Sometimes it's easier to step outside of yourself to get a different perspective so that you can develop awareness more effectively. In this section we'll work with several exercises that enable you to shift into the state of awareness if it isn't one that is familiar to you.

### AWARENESS EXERCISE PART ONE
### SITTING NEXT TO YOURSELF:

For this exercise you are going to imagine a perfect copy of yourself, sitting or standing just to your right. Take a deep breath, and relax into whatever space you are occupying at this moment. Next, mentally envision this perfect copy of yourself just to your right. Envision it sitting there quietly and observing your surroundings. The screen that you're looking at. The people around you. The smells in the room. It notices the air on your body. It even sees your thoughts (even though it is thought-less, itself). It observes emotions and feelings too. What you're thinking at this moment about this experience, what you're thinking about this imaginary being sitting next to you—it is observing you. It sees it all. It cuts through it all.

When you become aware by seeing the world through the eyes of this imaginary being, it can start to shift you into another realm. You are seeing yourself thinking, rather than being the thinker. Everything becomes more electric, as your awareness is finely tuned to this moment. Zen Buddhists equate this feeling to the luminosity and clarity that exists under water. It is the quietness of being, and the freshness of each moment. This is what this space of awareness feels like, and it's what the world looks like through the eyes of your perfect self. You're simply the observer of this world around you; you don't operate from automation.

The more you practice this exercise, the more you are able to be aware of being aware. Instead of hiding behind yesterday's memories and tomorrow's dreams, you move beyond them to now.

The opposite of this awakened mind is the reality that most of us normally experience. Just like when we go to the movies and we see images that make sense to us, we are actually watching electrons dancing on the screen. We do the same in our own, daily reality—we see the movement on the surface of reality and we mistake it for that which is real.

To be truly aware, and present in this moment, you have to opt out of this continuous loop of a movie that almost everyone is in. The choice is to watch with the same eyes as the perfect being who sits beside you, so you become an observer of your world rather than a zombie within it.

It's worth noting that, as we develop these practices, they are unlike a lot of meditation teachings in the Western world, which are designed to create mental clarity or sustained attention, often so you can function better at work or keep up with an intensive routine. For example, a 2010 *Psychological Science* study by MacLean et al.,[4] titled "Intensive meditation training improves perceptual discrimination and sustained attention," showed how meditation benefits us in this way. However, *mental clarity is more like an* <u>*outcome*</u> *of true meditation practice than the final destination.* Mental clarity and sustained attention aren't the awareness itself. We might feel clearer in mind and body, but it doesn't mean that we are embodying some of the traits of spiritual awakening, such as compassion, love, connection, peace, etc. This understanding is essential for Artemes because we are not just

meditating and developing awareness for our own growth. We are using these practices to further embody the qualities associated with spiritual awakening, and use them to contribute to social evolution.

## WORKING WITH YOUR FEAR

There can be a kind of fear that can arise when you begin awakening. It's the fear that comes with no longer conforming to a reality that you had become accustomed to. This fear can be off-putting. We've talked about how many of us would rather stay comfy in the shells of the world we have created than really awaken. The fear can intensify when we feel the concepts that had been the foundation of our world slowly begin to crumble. All these ideals that we held true—from the nature of society, to our beliefs about capitalism or socialism, to our sense of family and self—all these can start to fall apart, which can feel scary at times. We start to question the relationships around us, and those that have been taken for granted begin to change as we no longer conform to our roles. We start to see through the dream, so that at the same time we see how we are all connected, how we are all confused, how we have all been fucked up, and how we are all perfect too. We lose the desire to prove ourselves or be greater than another and we start to see equality, where before we had seen competition. All the identities that we had held to be so precious begin to fade away and we realize, often with great shock and wonder, "I am just not who I thought I was." There is a great urge to move forward into the unknown, but there is also often resistance, as these old identities, and the benefits that go with them, can act to pull us back in the direction of who we once were.

Getting beyond that fear requires an honest reckoning of what you gain from your old egoskeleton. Usually you are clinging to some old part of yourself because there is some kind of payoff, and in order to get beyond the fear, you have to ask yourself what it is you fear losing. Once you can get past that point, and deeply own the payoffs of the roles you have played so far, you reach a whole new level of self-realization where you are choosing moment by moment, rather than reacting to your preconditioned roles.

## GLOBAL AWARENESS

As you already know, the Artemes Training isn't just designed so that you can become a more fulfilled individual. We are also working towards the part you play in humanity's evolution. So your awareness needs to extend beyond the personal, otherwise you'll awaken as an individual but then, so what? We need to ensure we ground your awareness in your contribution to the whole. This piece can be equally as challenging as your personal awakening, because it involves recognizing and owning behaviors that exploit other people (or the environment) when you are checked out from reality.

For example, if you have a habit of checking out and buying a ton of clothes when you don't actually need them, are you willing to allow an awareness of the impact or consequences of that behavior? Are you willing to look at the environmental impact of this habit? What about the possible exploitation of those who have been involved in making the clothes? This level of awakening requires us to open our eyes in a completely different way to the world that has become socially acceptable to us, and this may cost us more than

our comforting behaviors. It may impact our careers too. A friend of mine shared a recent conversation he had with his sister in California who was giving up her high-level corporate job to become a Certified Functional Medicine Health Coach. "The corporate lifestyle just got out of control. There was no awareness in the direction that we were heading. The culture just didn't make sense to me anymore. I had to change, for myself." The courage she showed to give up her benefits (a comfortable life in San Francisco where she was well-paid to play her role in the dream), and to take risks to live true beyond those rewards—that's the kind of courage we are looking for with awareness. To see beyond personal gain to global impact. To make choices based on what we know is true, and not based on what is socially acceptable or what everyone else is doing. That's the kind of behavior it takes to create change on a global scale and the choice that is open to all of us.

You don't need to be a high-level corporate employee in San Francisco to see the price of your choices. Any of us who have any kind of privilege need to be willing to shine awareness on the different ways we are willing to exploit others. For those who press play on a porn movie: are they taking into consideration the industry they are supporting and the level of exploitation that many of the people in the sex industry are subjected to—or do they just press play? More than 5,517,748,800 hours of porn were watched on Porn Hub in 2018, which is equal to 629,880 years of content consumed in one year.[5] And that's just one porn site. For those who buy the latest exotic fruit—did they stop to consider the working conditions of the pickers? These are the kinds of questions we need to be willing to ask ourselves with awareness, especially if our automated behaviors involve goods or services created by others.

These issues can be even closer to home. Statistics say that over 40 percent of food in America is wasted.[6] This amounts to $162 billion in annual waste (and if you remember from chapter 3, we could solve the world hunger epidemic with $30 billion per year). If you throw away your food while stepping over a guy who is begging for food in the street; if you buy organic food for your dog and on your trip to the grocery store ignore the homeless woman that asks you for help; you're carrying out all these behaviors because you've been entrained to respond in a way that says they are OK. If we step back with awareness and look at the way we are socially conditioned to behave, some of our responses are so divorced from our sense of compassion that when we open our eyes to them, it's barely believable that they are seen as OK.

I call out these behaviors not to bring you to a sense of shame. An essential part of the work is to bring about awareness that creates change in your behavior rather than you feeling like something is wrong with you. If we all open our eyes wide to the ways the world around us operates, then each of us, one by one, can take responsibility from that place so that we start moving the world in the direction of more equality and consciousness.

## SUMMING UP

The first step in the Artemes journey is opening to awareness. Many traditional spiritual paths have awareness as a central focus. The majority of those paths place individual awareness as the main goal of the practice so that we can wake up to the automatic programs and learned behaviors that have been running our lives so far. Individual awareness is a core part of the Artemes Training, but in addition, it is also focused on the awakening of humanity as a whole.

### We looked at how:

- If you want to awaken, you can't face that hurdle with the same mechanical approach that you've likely used for other things. It's not "10 steps and it's done."

- If you are resistant to the process, it won't work. You have to put in consistent effort to wake up.

- The truth is that most of us don't actually want to be aware. The majority of us only truly want awareness in the areas that it suits or benefits us, and are prepared to ignore the areas where we still gain comfort and security.

- Many of us choose to ignore, or turn our awareness away from, the habits, the issues and the challenges that keep us locked in our individual identities.

- The truth is that our society is set up so that we continuously fall asleep.

- Awareness requires you to be:
  - Brutally honest with yourself.
  - Willing to face where you are asleep at the wheel.
  - Aware of the conflicting thoughts or emotions.
  - Aware of the roles that you play.

- There can be a kind of fear that can arise when you begin awakening. It's the fear that comes with no longer conforming to a reality that you had become accustomed to.

- Getting beyond that fear requires an honest reckoning of what you gain from keeping your old egoskeleton.

- Artemes Training isn't just designed so that you can become a more fulfilled individual. Your awareness needs to extend beyond the personal; otherwise you'll awaken as an individual, but then, so what? We are also working towards creating the part you play in humanity's evolution.

Now that we have defined awareness as an essential component to your personal awakening, and rooted your awareness in the goal of waking up so you can benefit both yourself and humanity, we'll move into two parts of your human experience that often block awareness. In the next chapter we will look at how you can navigate thoughts to develop more awareness, and in the chapter that follows we'll look at how you can navigate emotions to support your awakening.

# CHAPTER SEVEN
## NAVIGATING THOUGHT

One of the primary objectives of the Artemes Training is to develop your relationship with thought.

The name Artemes comes from the thoughts we have—that come like arrows—when we are in a state of conscious awareness. These are the conscious and creative thoughts that come from beyond our programming and beliefs, and they are essential to our evolution as humanity. These thoughts emerge from a different part of the brain than those which come from fear. These creative, aware, and expansive thoughts are the ones that will allow us to envision a new version of reality and forge forward to overcome the many and varied challenges of our human existence. The Artemes System came from this place and is my own contribution to humanity in these times. Yet I am just one among many. Now imagine what will occur when millions of us all around the world have shifted our brains to operating from awareness. Picture what kind of world we would be living in if we were all operating from conscious thought.

So the aim of the Artemes System is for each individual to take responsibility for operating from that place so that we can collectively evolve humanity to a state of consciousness where we exist in the higher realms of our human potential. Where peace, love, compassion, and understanding elevate us above hate, destruction, self-centeredness and competition. Each of us can develop these higher centers of our brain, and much of the work we do with Artemes is created so that we operate from this place. However, we also recognize that the majority—if not all—of us have been programmed into a different version of reality through our collective unconscious training. In order to operate from conscious thought, we must also recognize and learn to work with the psychological programming that holds us in the old paradigm of reality that we are working to move beyond.

Artemes is therefore working on two levels when it comes to upgrading your consciousness. One is to develop practices that enable you to cultivate conscious thought. The other is to develop tools that enable you to recognize when outdated mental patterns have been activated, so that you can work to rewire your brain. In this chapter we'll be addressing the challenging thoughts that take you out of the present moment first, and developing the context for conscious thought second. We are presenting these sequentially; however, it's recommended that you work on these two practices simultaneously so that you are cultivating conscious thought while working with any mental hijacks that present themselves in your mind.

## The Many Faces of Thought

A friend of mine experienced a thought-based (as opposed to awareness-based) reality when her husband told her he was no longer in love with her, and hadn't been for some time. She lay sobbing in the fetal position for more than two weeks.

Several weeks later, we walked together through the countryside and she shared the agony of her experience. After letting her know I felt empathy for her experience, I asked if I could question her to help her see things differently. When she agreed, I asked her, "Why are you letting thoughts create hell for you in this moment?"

We experimented with separating the beauty of the moment from the thoughts that are based in the past. I told her that at this moment everything was perfect, but instead of experiencing this perfection, she was experiencing the hell of an abstract past.

A light bulb of awareness was switched on in her reality, and in that moment, she awoke from the pain. She was able to separate herself from the hell that she was experiencing in herself. She saw how that hell was created in her head, and not in reality. She understood that it was fine to hurt over her predicament when it was actually happening, but that it was also fine to leave that behind when it wasn't her current moment of reality.

A few years have passed since this meeting. She got a divorce, and she is happier than she has ever been. She has continued on her path of awakening, is becoming stronger and stronger each day, and is even mentoring her ex-husband on how to separate reality from thought. She took the pain of the end of a marriage as a catalyst for waking up and separating herself from her overall pain.

(It's worth noting that in the story above, my friend was receptive to seeing things differently and I worked carefully to make sure that I respected where she was, while simultaneously offering her a different view on reality. Particularly when we are new to the spiritual path, it's essential that we learn to simultaneously honor the thought-based hell that others are experiencing, while offering them a different path.)

The example above is just one type of thought that can lead to a destructive reality. We've already highlighted that all of our thoughts are not created equally, and some are destructive in nature while others are expansive. Some types of thinking include:

**Compulsive thinking** - These are the thoughts that just go around and around in your head, like you are chewing gum with your mind. These usually don't contain any emotional or fear-based thoughts. They contain things like endless lists of things done in the past or things to do, mental rehearsals (what I'm going to say in this future situation), mental recapping (rethinking of non-emotive memories), etc. They are the thoughts that drift aimlessly throughout your waking hours, using up mental energy and keeping you out of the present, but not impacting your emotional state.

**Mental hijacking** - These are the destructive thoughts that are generated from fear, anger, jealousy, anxiety, rage, and so on. They literally act like terrorists hijacking your mind. Usually these thoughts are accompanied by a

change in your emotional climate and a chemical reaction, such as adrenalin.

**Creative thinking** - This is where you move out of thinking for the sake of it and use your mind to create and solve problems. This kind of thinking usually only occurs when you are not in the hijack phase. (When you are triggered into fear or anger, the creative aspects of your brain usually shut down.)

**Conscious thought** - These are the thoughts that arise from conscious awareness. Unlike the empty thoughts that bounce aimlessly around our heads, these thoughts come from a meditative space. They appear to me as arrows of thought projected from a void.

We'll be working very practically to reduce the compulsive thinking and mental hijacking, while simultaneously developing the arena for conscious and creative thought to be fostered.

## Reducing Compulsive Thinking

For thousands of years and in pretty much every language and religion, there has been material written on the nature of thought. Over the past couple of decades, the notion that we can be the observer of our thought has been absorbed into popular spiritual culture.

The understanding that most of us are asleep—hypnotized by our past experience and the voices in our heads that narrate our reality—has become a popular perspective in the spiritual realm. The reality that it describes is a continuous loop of past memories (good and bad) and future dreams (good and bad). Many of the modern "positive thinking" techniques fall short of interrupting this loop because we are taught that we must continuously eradicate negative thought, and only focus on the positive. This has created a great number of individuals obsessed with positive thinking. However, if you just focus on positive thoughts, you are still caught in the same reality trap of your thoughts—it just has a different flavor. The deeper work is to see all compulsive thinking as a trap, whether "positive" or "negative." To wake up, you must break free of the idea that you are a product of your past experience and of the voice in your head. The voice in your head can jab and cut better than Muhammad Ali. Awareness protects us from the blows.

Daydreaming is a form of socially acceptable compulsive thinking. It's usually a fantasy of what might be or a memory of what has gone before. It exhausts our resources and keeps us out of the present moment. The tools that we began to develop in the previous chapter around awareness will enable you to shine a light on your compulsive thinking behaviors. As you become aware of being aware, you will hear the voices that you constantly reproduce inside of you. Maybe you will recognize themes and patterns which you repeat over and over again. The main objective is to observe yourself without judgment, because when you wake yourself up in these moments, when you really see the constant themes that you reproduce over and over again on a moment-by-moment basis, it can feel like you are going crazy for a while. It helps to remember that you are just like everyone else! Your brain is an incredibly powerful tool that gets wired with experiences, and up until now, you may not have been given the tools or processes to wire it in a way so you can use it to its most effective capacity. No judgment or blame. Just a commitment to upgrading, and a lot of humor, as you notice the absurdity of the way we have been socially and culturally

trained to misuse one of the most incredible gifts we have been given, and how with consistency and awareness we can rewire the brain to remain present and in the moment.

## Mental Hijack

There's a woman with one eye who hangs out by my local dollar store. She wears overalls and looks both edgy and interesting at the same time—like an actress portraying a mechanic in a 1970s B flick. Every once in a while, she'll find a piece of cardboard and write "Anything you can spare is greatly appreciated. God bless." For some reason she scares the shit out of people.

Recently I saw a guy pull up to the stop sign where she was standing, notice her, and slam his foot on the accelerator, nearly causing a pileup on the road.

It's in moments such as this that we need to pause and ask ourselves what we are actually afraid of.

Our minds create stories that are based upon everything that we have experienced up to this moment in our life, including books, documentaries, horror flicks, sci-fi films, all those rabbit holes of YouTube videos, and every conversation you've ever had with your mom, dad, preacher, and teacher.

It's from these experiences that your mind creates stories of fear that are projected onto the innocent.

- "I don't trust that lady," (based upon watching *Fight Club* ten years ago)
- "I bet she's on drugs," (based upon a conversation with your aunt Helen when you were thirteen years old)
- "Lock the doors, Bunnie!" (based upon watching *Escape from New York* in 2nd grade)
- "Where does she get the nerve?" (based upon reading *Archetypes and the Collective Unconscious* a few years ago)
- "She's wearing nicer overalls than I am," (based upon your fears that you aren't enough).

The voice in our head spouts these things out as if they were reality. Our mind then creates a movie that matches the voice perfectly. Just as when we're sound asleep in bed at night and we experience ourselves being chased by a dog, we don't know that this experience is dreaming. At this moment, it is reality! This only happens in our heads, but we react to it in our external reality.

Previously I referred to the shell that we have built up around our existence as the egoskeleton, and the first crack in breaking this is the willingness to accept that any thought that arises may not be true.

Most of us have experienced being hijacked by thought at some point in our lives, and for many of us, this occurs on a weekly, or even daily, basis. Sometimes a memory triggers a mental hijack, other times a situation in your external reality will cause one to arise. In the chapter that follows this one, we'll be working with emotional triggers, so for this chapter we are mainly focusing on those mental hijacks that come out of nowhere and cause you to obsess at 1,000 miles an hour, taking

you out of your center, often catapulting you into rage and other non-centering emotions. It also includes catastrophic thinking, where you suddenly spiral into personal and social doomsday scenarios, picturing the end of your life or the end of humanity. Yet dark times are sometimes exactly what's needed to push you into the light.

## Red Train

Your mental hijacks often feel like you have jumped on a "red train" and are hurtling towards an unknown destiny at 1,000 miles an hour.

### RED TRAIN EXERCISE :

A simple strategy you can use: as soon as you identify yourself as being on a "red train" of thought, you wake yourself up with awareness by saying, "I'm on a red train," followed by the question, "Am I willing to jump off?" You can visualize or imagine yourself jumping off this train so that you are no longer getting dragged along by it. There will likely be some afterthoughts as your mind tries to hang onto what you were obsessing about and as your body chemistry adjusts to your choice, but fundamentally this exercise reminds you that you have the power to disrupt your thoughts, and that you are the one who is in control.

If you get triggered into red train thinking, often one of the outcomes is to find something that numbs the pain (whether it's porn, beers at the local bar, bingeing on chicken wings, *Call of Duty*, retail therapy or whatever your personal poison is). In the previous chapter we started to break down your actions so that you recognize your distracting or compulsive behaviors. Now, going one step further, you need to work on facing them. Be the observer of the way your brain fires off in these moments and the body chemistry that accompanies it. See if you can laugh with yourself in the middle of it all as you catch the familiar pattern. With time, awareness, and consistent practice (plus the accompanying work exercises we are going to do in the chapter that follows on emotions), you will begin to master these states so that (a) they diminish in frequency and (b) when they do arise, they don't have the same power over you because you have worked on breaking them down.

## Cultivating Conscious Thought

Artemes is the space where open awareness and creative thought dance. If you are locked in the past or obsessing about the future all the time, you will rarely (if ever) experience that space. Many remarkable individuals have found a way to reach that space without spiritual practice. Across time, poets, musicians, artists, and revolutionaries have found a way to access this space. So, in addition to working with your compulsive, catastrophic thinking and mental hijacks, there is also the practice of cultivating a space where conscious thoughts develop.

All thoughts come out of space. Like a stone skipping across flat water, presence comes in a pitter-patter kind of way. In the beginning, awareness occurs only briefly—you feel the cool water, but quickly you're back in the air. As you practice, your moments in the air

will become much less prolonged and your time in the cool water of awareness will increase until you are totally enveloped. For this reason, it's essential to develop your relationship with space in order to cultivate a climate that fosters conscious thought. Most of us don't think about our relationship to space. In the material paradigm that we operate in, it is objects that we fixate upon. Some of these objects can be:

- Material—what we buy or acquire
- Sound—what we hear
- Thoughts—what we think (past and future)
- People—relationships and who we interact with.

All these are the "stuff" of our life, and because society slants our reality towards this materially-oriented world, we have been well trained to focus on them. Very rarely, if ever at all, are we taught to focus on the space between these things. When we focus on the space, it means putting our attention to:

- Material—the space around the objects that we see
- Sound—the gap in between what we hear
- Thoughts—the pause between our thoughts
- People—the space that exists between us and another.

We look around and see objects everywhere: trees, houses, chairs, birds, light posts, and so on. In addition to these seemingly solid structures, there is also the space that we move within. Just as solid objects are made up of elements from the universe, this seemingly empty space is as well. Instead of a universe of emptiness with sporadic lumps of solidified elements (which most of us would assume), the entire universe is instead a wholly-connected and seamless entity unto itself.

For an object to be created, there must be space. The tree cannot exist without space. The horse cannot gallop without space. Without space, nothing is possible. Space is the thing that has never changed and it has always been here. The only way to experience this space is to shift your awareness to existing within it.

Switching your awareness from the material to space can literally be one of the most transforming exercises you do. From a biological standpoint, when you focus on the space rather than the objects, a powerful switch takes place in your nervous system. If you walk down the streets of a busy city such as Los Angeles—and you are focusing on the people, the traffic, the noise—your nervous system will likely become overstimulated very quickly, which is why a lot of people will say they get overwhelmed in cities. But you can walk down the same street with your focus on the space in between everything, and you will feel something inside you switch. You are not focusing on the content of the city and all the objects that you interact with. Instead you are focusing on the space between those objects and moving through that space. It sends a completely different signal to your nervous system and with a little practice, you can instantly feel much calmer.

You don't need to be in the extremes of LA to practice this exercise. It can be practiced in any setting (I especially enjoy doing it in nature), in order to heighten your sense of being present.

## DEVELOPING AWARENESS OF SPACE:

1. Start by observing the objects in your surroundings. No need to label anything, just notice the content around you. Just be here and observe without needing to narrate. Look at your couch, your table, but resist the urge to tell yourself, "There is the couch, there is the table." Just see them.

2. Pick out one object in your field of view (your computer maybe). Take two deep breaths and while doing this, really focus on the object, again with no story about it (a story would be, "My screen needs cleaning," or "Next year I'll get a new computer.") Just see it without narrating it. Simply let it be as it is.

3. Next, select another object that you can see within the same field of view (it can be a wall, a water bottle, or anything else that you see). Take two deep breaths and get to know this object in the same way as you did the first one. Again, no story. Just see it.

4. Now place your focus on the space between the two objects. So if you were looking at the computer and the wall, look at the space between them. Relax your gaze (so you are not looking at anything in particular). Simply feel the space that exists between the two objects.

5. Next, expand this awareness to all the space that exists around your two objects, and then all the space in your view. Now, only observe space, letting the two objects and every other object fade away to the background. See and feel the space. And notice what shifts inside you when you do.

"Seeing" space is often accompanied by an experience of something shifting inside you. When I first began to exist in this space, I had the experience of moving beyond pleasure and pain, beyond good and evil, to just being. Instead of muddling through the content of my life, exhausted by moving from one thing to the next, I started to feel myself existing in a space of open awareness where life made much more sense. There, I was more of an observer, a consciousness, rather than the identity I had falsely believed myself to be before. My fake persona that I had left behind was created by society, and by my desperate need to know my place and fit in. From within the space, I could see where I had played a role and been a fraud. I saw how those around me were playing their roles too. They were perfect but at the same time, fucked up by their roles, like me. As I saw the game that we were all playing, a love of all humanity came over me. I saw for the first time how each of us is just the product of the situation we are placed in. It wasn't that thought that set me free, but more the sense that I could finally see the choice that we all have.

## Taking the Space Exercise Out on the Streets

Once you have practiced this exercise in your home, you can start to use it in your everyday reality. Again, one of the best places to use it is in nature or out in the streets. If you use it in nature, it's going to heighten your experience of being outside. If you use it on the streets, especially in busy cities, it's going to give you a tool to navigate both your thoughts and your nervous system differently.

## WALKING SPACE:

1. Start by feeling your feet hit the ground as you walk. Fully "articulate" your feet. In other words, take steps where the whole of your foot rolls on the ground, heel to toe, driving your feet into the ground. Feel the sensation on your feet. Really notice the ground from here.

2. Still feeling your feet on the ground, imagine there is a hand on your back, between your shoulder blades, supporting you. As you do, notice all the content around you. The sounds, the objects, the people, and so on. So now you are in the content of everything around you.

3. Still feeling your feet on the ground and the imaginary hand on your back, look out at the horizon in front of you and now de-focus your eyes so you are no longer looking at the objects and people, but you are focusing on the space in between them. Whenever you get distracted, say to yourself, "Feet on the ground, hand on the back, horizon, space in between things," so you constantly keep bringing yourself back to the space and moving through that.

You will notice, with practice, that this exercise changes the way you think and feel about moving through crowds (or nature). It will change your presence and awareness, and deeply impact the way your nervous system expresses itself. With regular practice it is likely that a sense of ease will inhabit you.

## SUMMING UP

One of the primary objectives of the Artemes System is to develop your relationship with thought.

### We looked at how:

- The name Artemes comes from the thoughts—that come like arrows—which we receive when we are in a state of conscious awareness.

- These are the conscious and creative thoughts that come from beyond our programming and beliefs, and they are essential to our evolution as humanity.

- Some types of thinking include:
  - **Compulsive thinking** - The thoughts that just go around and around in your head, like you are chewing gum with your mind. All compulsive thinking, whether "positive" or "negative," is a trap. To wake up, you must break free of the idea that you are a product of your past experience and the voice in your head.

  - **Mental hijacking** - These are the destructive thoughts that are generated from fear, anger, jealousy, anxiety, rage, and so on. The voice in our head carries on as if it were reality. Our mind then creates a movie that matches the voice perfectly. This often spirals into catastrophic

thinking and doomsday scenarios.

○ **Creative thinking** - This is where you move out of thinking for the sake of it and use your mind to create and solve problems.

○ **Conscious thought** - These are the thoughts that arise from conscious awareness, and the thoughts that come from the space of being aware. We can move into conscious thought by paying attention to the space in between the "stuff" in our life.

Now that we've taken a look at the thoughts in our head, and how we can shape our thinking to experience more consciousness, in the chapter that follows we'll look at our emotional triggers, and how we can work with them—particularly in the chaos of these current times—to remain more present.

# CHAPTER EIGHT
## NAVIGATING EMOTIONS

Our core goal with Artemes is to create a system that supports humanity to return to more compassion, peace, love, connection, fairness, and understanding. The conscious economic system of Artemes was designed to close socio-economic gaps and create a fairer distribution of wealth for some of the challenges that humanity collectively faces, and the members of the Council of the Aware are chosen because they embody these values.

The Artemes System, therefore, supports emotional development on a twofold path. In one aspect, you develop peace, compassion, kindness, and love for other human beings so that you take action to contribute to our world in a way that makes a difference to others. In the other aspect, you develop these qualities within yourself for your own growth. This includes developing the emotional intelligence to recognize when your

emotional reactions and responses to your environment and the people around you are taking you out of the present moment, and developing strategies to effectively understand and navigate your emotional triggers.

In this chapter we'll be supporting you to develop an understanding of why your emotions get triggered, and we'll be providing you with tools and strategies to work with those triggers so they are reduced in intensity, frequency, and duration. In the chapter that follows, we'll be working to cultivate more of the "higher qualities" of peace, love, joy, and compassion so that they become more of a predominant state for you as you progress through your life.

## Understanding the Brain

In order to navigate our emotions effectively, we first need to have an overview of how the different parts of our brain work together. This is eloquently highlighted in *Brain Wash*, by doctors David and Austin Perlmutter, MD.[1] In summary, we have our:

- **Original brain**, which dates back to the time that we were reptiles. Housed in the brainstem, it regulates "heartbeat, breathing, blood pressure, circulation, digestion, and the famous fight and flight response."[2] It's the instinctual part of our brain that regulates survival.

- **Limbic brain**, which "sits on top of the brainstem and receives input from the old reptilian brain below." The limbic brain is the emotional generator. Its responses are reflexive, "without conscious analysis, reflection, or interpretation." One of the key elements of the limbic brain is the amygdala, which is "the control center for the threat-response and threat interpretation system." The amygdala is the part of the brain that records our life-threatening experiences and creates an early warning system if it perceives that we are about to have a similar experience. The amygdala regulates our emotions and impulsivity. It is seen as "an essential part of the story that has led us to our current societal predicament."[3] However, most relevant to the Artemes System is the fact that the amygdala is in communication with the other parts of the brain—in particular, the prefrontal cortex.

- **Third Brain,** which is the cerebral cortex—the part of the brain that is most recent in human evolution. It is this 'newer' part of the brain that gives us the ability to "think analytically and logically, problem solve, plan for the future, and think abstractly." It regulates the responses of the older parts of the brain. The cerebral cortex is described as "reflective, contemplative, and methodical." One of the key elements of the cerebral cortex is the prefrontal cortex, which is unique to humans.

## The Relationship Between the Amygdala and the Prefrontal Cortex

Of most significance to the Artemes System is the relationship between the amygdala and the prefrontal cortex. While the prefrontal cortex allows us to weigh up alternatives, the amygdala reacts with

impulsivity. As doctors David and Austin Perlmutter highlight, "Without the supervision of the prefrontal cortex, there is no adult in the room." When the amygdala is running the show, "the emotionally immature child can run amok, lacking rules, discipline, and boundaries."[4]

The relationship between the amygdala and the prefrontal cortex is so significant for Artemes because much of the work that we are doing in our system of awakening—particularly when it comes to emotions— can be described as creating a better relationship between these two parts of the brain. Up until this point in life, you may have experienced many moments where your amygdala took over. In fact, many of the experiences where we suddenly react from our unconscious are based on the reaction of the amygdala. In all the work that we do in Artemes, we are developing the prefrontal cortex so that we are conscious and responsive, rather than unconscious and reactive. We need to develop an awareness of when the amygdala has been triggered into a reaction, so that we can calm it with the reasoning of the prefrontal cortex.

But it isn't just our individual responses that are affected by developing our prefrontal cortex. It's the way that we respond to the planet too. In *Brain Wash*, we learn what you may have already instinctively realized yourself, i.e., that "people with relatively inactive prefrontal cortices may be less concerned about the planet's health than others are. They are, simply put, selfish in every sense of the word—from the way they treat others to the way they treat the environment." In contrast, actively engaging the prefrontal cortex "makes us more compassionate and empathic as individuals."[5] This understanding has massive implications for the work that we are doing as social evolutionaries within the

Artemes System. It explains how the cryptocurrency system with the Council of the Aware goes hand in hand with our own spiritual development. The more we practice the tools and exercises that are presented in the Artemes System, the more we develop our prefrontal cortex, and the more we naturally want to contribute to being more socially responsible beings who care for the plight of humanity.

## Emotional Indicators

So, you can measure your spiritual growth by the way you treat and respond to others. If your spiritual growth path is just centered on yourself, you'll feel awesome until you encounter a challenge with someone, and then you'll drop out of your higher qualities of peace, compassion, and kindness, and into the qualities of the amygdala, such as anger, rage, indignation or self-righteousness in order to respond to that challenge.

Some spiritual paths reject emotions altogether, and even go so far as to see other human beings as an inconvenience to the spiritual growth path. In the Artemes Training we are developing ourselves so that we make a more effective contribution to the whole. Although Artemes is a path of nonself-judgment, we can evaluate how far we have come by our emotional reactions to others.

This does not mean that we will never be firm, strong or clear. In fact, the opposite is true. On some paths a kind of spiritual cliché has developed, which seems to suggest the aim of spirituality is to operate from a one-dimensional emotional tone all of the time. This stereotype would never raise their voice, and would address every challenge with

a softly spoken tone. In the Artemes System, we eliminate this cliché because it is based on a false belief about how someone on a spiritual path should behave, and because it springs from the misinformed assumption that spirituality is about eradicating the more challenging emotions. In Artemes, all your emotions are welcomed and integrated. It's not that you are required to eradicate anger, fear, sadness or grief. It's that you develop tools and processes to navigate them differently, recognizing your triggers and creating a healthier communication between the amygdala and prefrontal cortex.

Particularly in this current climate, there may be circumstances that require you to be firm, to call others out, to challenge prejudice or to take affirmative action. As we collectively work to break down some of the issues we face globally today, such as racism, sexism, ableism, classism, xenophobia, homophobia, and prejudice towards immigrants and refugees, and as we begin to bring to the forefront some of the issues we have ignored, such as socio-economic disparity, prison reform and environmental challenges, there may be instances where we absolutely need to be firm and direct. The difference is, in the Artemes System, we work towards doing this from a place where we have processed our own anger and other consuming emotions, so that we do not add fuel to the fire with what we are feeling, and so that we are contributing from beyond our own survival responses. It is from this space that a true synergy between all forces (some of which were previously labeled as "opposing," but now we know are one) will create the change that humanity needs in this moment to move forward.

## Learning to Navigate Emotions

The two main factors that take us out of the present moment are our thoughts and our emotional triggers. In the previous chapter we explored different ways to work with your thoughts so that you catch yourself spiraling into destructive thought patterns, and change the course of your thinking. In this chapter we will explore a similar approach with your emotions.

We don't attempt to reject or eliminate any of our emotional responses, but instead, we learn to ride the wave of them differently. This eventually leads to being able to be present with whatever emotions arise without necessarily reacting from *within* that emotion.

If you are alive and human, chances are that you've experienced being overwhelmed by your emotions at some point. Most of us have reacted with outrage, indignation, anger or hostility enough to know that it can feel utterly destructive to ourselves and others when we do. We've all felt those highs of reacting and the lows that follow when we trigger a cascade of chemicals in an inflammatory emotional response. And while it's already been highlighted that the goal is not to become emotionally flat, having the tools to make choices to disrupt that process can be empowering, changing the course of how you respond in a variety of situations. From that place, you still might decide to challenge, disrupt, and call out someone else's behavior, but it will have a totally different flavor once you've been through the Artemes Training, because you'll be *responding* rather than *reacting*.

## Emotions and Survival

Perhaps one of the key things to understanding your emotional responses is that they are closely linked to your survival mechanisms. As was mentioned earlier, each of us has a component in our brain that has been with us since early on in our evolution. Although much of the work with Artemes is to develop the higher centers of our brain, understanding how emotions get triggered, and the disconnect this can create from these higher centers is essential to your awakening, and it all begins with the survival response.

If you've ever lost your shit about something when the person next to you remained calm, or experienced the opposite—found yourself confused about why someone else is freaking out over something so trivial—it can help to understand that our emotional reactions are learned, and based on our life experiences. This is great news in relation to the Artemes Training, because it means that they can be unlearned too.

Our life experiences—particularly the stressful or traumatic ones—become imprinted in our subconscious for a very specific reason. *Our subconscious mind is trying to protect us from experiencing something similar, so it creates a warning response, so that we don't repeat the same issues over and over again.* While most people assume that their emotions are working against them, the opposite is actually true, and our challenging emotions are triggered as responses in an attempt to protect us.

If we went through something big, our subconscious is going to trigger similar chemical responses and emotions to those we experienced at that time, which means a similar event—even if not dangerous—can trigger a cascade of chemical reactions that create an emotional response. We can be triggered by a smell, a taste, a sound, something we see, or something we touch. If the experience (or series of events) that we went through was severe, it can mean we get triggered into a fight, flight or freeze response on multiple occasions, and this can severely impact our perception and our responses in our everyday reality. It creates a distorted filter through which we see the world, and we keep responding to perceived threats, even when they aren't actually real.

Unless we find a way to process the information that is held on a subconscious level relating to stressful or traumatic events that we experienced in the past, we can find ourselves reliving those events over and over again. How you integrate these parts of your story will be crucial in enabling you to break down these automated emotional responses so you can switch your consciousness on even when you are triggered into an overwhelming feeling. We need to resolve these triggers so we don't keep reliving the events of the past.

## Survival Responses

We've mentioned survival in a number of different contexts in this book, and that's because our survival is at the heart of everything. Understanding that almost all of our difficult emotional responses come from our desire to survive is one of the first steps in the evolution of our emotions.

A friend of mine once told me about an experience she had when she visited a spiritual commune in California. She was sitting around a table with a group of spiritual practitioners talking about the film *Alive*, which was based on the story of a group of plane crash survivors who were forced to eat the bodies of those who had died in the crash in order to survive. One of the practitioners at the table told her, "If I ever found myself in such a situation, I hope I would choose to dip out much more gracefully." My friend challenged his point of view, for a very specific reason. She knew that when we are triggered into survival, it makes us behave differently. Someone who has lived a life where they have never experienced true hunger, food insecurity, lack of resources, or a true threat to their life, can easily be fooled into believing they are immune to the survival response. But when that response kicks in, it shuts down the higher centers of the brain so we start to behave differently. It does that because we are uniquely wired to survive. Many of the people experiencing homelessness on our streets behave in certain ways because they are operating from a permanent state of survival. We need to develop compassion for this state in others, and see how it is a driving force for many challenging behaviors, and to understand it in ourselves, too.

This response is not just unique to hunger. Survival can be traced back to nearly all the challenging emotions that you feel.

Think of jealousy. I once spent weeks not talking to my partner because jealousy was triggered within me. Yet jealousy is actually a survival response. It comes from fear of loss. When we lived in tribes, if we were rejected from the pack, we were alone and we did not survive. These primal responses get triggered in relationships because to survive as humans we had to be connected to the tribe (and even those of us who believe ourselves to be uniquely independent are overlooking the fact that we exist within a social structure, maybe taking for granted the input from others that support us in unseen ways). So the jealousy we feel is partly due to our evolutionary responses, then coupled with previous experiences we may have had which have made us feel unsafe in relationships. The cascade of emotions that are triggered due to our survival response and experiences make us behave in certain ways until we recognize and disrupt the patterns.

One of the challenges that survival creates is that it sets us up to compete against one another. In the US, we've been entrained with the mindset of "survival of the fittest." So we create a reality where we compete against one another rather than support one another to grow. Again, survival is at the heart of this behavior. If you think of the whole way our society is constructed so that we compete to be the most successful, beautiful, the hottest, strongest, and wealthiest, survival is actually at the heart of all of these seemingly superficial drives. Similarly, when we are threatened with illness, financial ruin, relationships ending, or anywhere we are losing something that feels essential to us, the survival trigger is activated.

If you think about many of the issues we collectively face as humanity, particularly the "isms" and prejudices including racism, sexism, homophobia, xenophobia, and Islamophobia, they stem from the fact that we have been *wrongly programmed to believe that there is a threat,* as that perceived threat is actually grounded in fear and misperception, rather than in truth. Anywhere we have created an "us" who are safe and a "them" who are a threat, we are operating from an outdated

survival mechanism based on our programming. We are often wrongly assuming there is something we need to protect ourselves against, and we do this because we want to survive.

When I look around me at my home in East Kentucky, where nearly a third of the people live below the poverty line or have food insecurities, I get to look survival in the face on an almost daily basis. You could say I'm one of the lucky ones, because although I was raised with financial challenges, I also had the skills, resources, and mindset that enabled me to break out of the survival poverty trap. One of the reasons I have stayed close to my home instead of leaving it all behind was that I had this overwhelming sense that I wanted to make the world around me better. I did this on a small scale by building a bar that was a center for my community in my earlier years. Today, creating Artemes is my approach to bridging this survival mechanism on a global scale. We need to ask ourselves how we can both individually and collectively break away from the survival mechanism so we are simultaneously doing so for ourselves, and creating opportunities for others to do so in the world around us.

When you understand how survival is at the heart of so many of the issues we collectively face, it changes the game exponentially. One of the goals of Artemes is to help more and more people break out of the emotional response of survival so that they can move into thriving. The conscious cryptocurrency system is the practical way that we do this, so that we create more economic opportunities for everyone to thrive more equally. But everyone that enters into Artemes needs to be able to navigate their own survival responses too. The challenge that we will be setting for you here is recognizing how your own survival response has been running the show so far.

## MEDITATING ON EMOTIONS:

As you put yourself in a meditative state, practice to isolate these emotions so that you can observe them and develop your emotional intelligence around how and when they arise. Ask yourself, "How does anger make me feel? Is it a tightness in the chest? A warming of the face?" "How about jealousy?" You can tune in with what came up in the past, mentally conjuring up what you perceive as the wrongs that have been done to you. Allow yourself to feel exactly what you feel and let that emotion pass through you. In your mind's eye, see if you can sense your prefrontal cortex (just above your eyes behind your forehead) and your amygdala (down near your brainstem) and create a connection between them, so that the higher centers of your brain can calm your emotional responses.

The next stage is to use the same exercise when you are emotionally triggered. Once you have practiced being with your emotions while on the mat, you will likely find that if you close your eyes when you are triggered, it is easier to wake yourself up and create a connection to the prefrontal cortex and the amygdala.

## Learning to Process Your Own Emotional Hijacks

In the US, we've learned to place far too much emphasis on how we feel. We've built a complete psychological system based on analyzing our feelings. We are taught and encouraged to express them as a form of self-empowerment, often to the detriment of others. What we are not so frequently taught to do is to assess where they are coming from

and why we are reacting to them, and to navigate them from beyond reacting to one another.

Some spiritual practices attempt to address this but fall short. Instead of processing emotions and dealing with them intelligently, some paths dismiss them or bypass them, so you end up with a surplus of suppressed energy, or a belief that you are dealing with emotional issues that have really just been pushed to the background. With Artemes, we learn to work with them, rather than reacting to them. We face our emotional hijacks and we develop ways to effectively process them so they are no longer running the show.

One of the core elements of the Artemes Training is developing strategies for when you are emotionally hijacked. This part of the training is carried out with a ton of self-compassion and understanding. If you want to deadlift weights, you wouldn't expect to start out at the highest weight. Strength training and weightlifting experts Mark Rippetoe and Lon Kilgore estimate that the average 198-pound male could lift 155 pounds even without training, but after a couple of years of proper training, that same lifter could likely deadlift 335 pounds.[6] You need to take a similar approach to dealing with your emotional hijacks.

No doubt, you know what it's like when your emotions have taken over. You are sailing through the day feeling switched on, connected, alive and free. And then something happens that triggers an emotional response. The chemicals in your body start to change. The adrenalin begins to pump, and before you know it, you don't recognize who you've become. At this point, many of us think we have failed at being human in some way. But the truth is, you are just acting from a chemical reaction that changes the structure of your brain and body chemistry. As you wake up more and more, you may notice that this chemical response still gets triggered—and if that happens, it doesn't mean you failed. However, what you learn to do is deal with it differently. You catch it before it spirals out of control. And you do this with awareness.

At first you might get all the way to the end of an emotional outburst before your awareness kicks in. But with practice, and over time, you learn to catch it earlier. So eventually you start to catch yourself before you react. Instead of speaking or acting from within your emotional response, you take yourself to one side. And this is the important piece that is missing from a lot of teachings about emotions. *You let yourself feel whatever you feel.* No judgment. No blaming yourself. No denying what you feel. No pushing it down. You just really sit with whatever is coming up for you. You follow Pema Chödrön's advice and you "lean into it." You let it be present inside you. And then, without forcing it or wishing it wasn't there, it passes through you. From there, you gain perspective and insight and if you need to take action, you can, but not from within the fire of the emotion.

So then the next time you get triggered, you may even catch yourself sooner, and eventually you will simultaneously feel the emotion arising and you will be able to wake yourself up from within that feeling. It's a core part of the Artemes Training and the main component is that it comes with a lot of compassion for yourself, knowing you've had a lifetime of being hijacked with no strategy. So you develop the tools to strategize your emotional responses, and eventually you can simultaneously get triggered and you hear a voice in your head saying something along the lines of, "Hold on for a moment, that's a massive chemical reaction. Something triggered you emotionally. Take a few breaths and get grounded and just be present to what you feel without reacting."

**HIJACK PLAN:** In what kinds of situations do you find yourself getting hijacked? What are the things that other people say or do (or that you say or do) that start this hijacking process? Get clear about what kinds of situations trigger anger, fear, jealousy, anxiety, and so on.

What surges in chemicals do you feel and what's your usual MO for these reactions?

- Avoidance – push the feelings away
- Outburst – explode and react
- Self-blame – judge yourself for how you are feeling

Create a strategy for waking yourself up in these moments. We've already been developing awareness in the exercises from the previous chapter, so look at how you can apply that here.

What kinds of scripts or reminders do you need in place when those surges come?

For example, "I say PAUSE inside my mind before I react," or "I take a deep breath and tell myself WAKE UP," or "I leave the room for a moment to compose myself."

The goal is to create a strategy (or a series of strategies for different situations) while you are not in the middle of the triggered moment, so that when you are hijacked, it gives you the best chance to take responsibility for your reaction.

Always bear in mind that because the higher centers of your brain get switched off when you are emotionally triggered, trying to think of a strategy when you are hijacked is almost impossible—you need to preplan what you are going to say and do.

The key is, whatever strategy you have in place, definitely don't plan to avoid how you feel by using alcohol, drugs, food or other distraction methods. Instead, learn to sit with whatever comes up, however uncomfortable it is, and practice just being with that feeling, even if it is overwhelming, teaching yourself to just be interested in whatever feelings or emotions you're experiencing. When you've learned to be with whatever comes up, it loses its edge on you, and it starts to change your reactions. It's like facing a monster that seemed way bigger than it actually is. The truth is, you are just learning to overcome your conditioned responses based on what you learned from those around you. You are regaining your power in an area where you have been programmed that your only power was to react. You are reframing your responses so you simultaneously allow yourself to feel whatever is present within you, and you navigate your responses in your external reality so you no longer feel like a puppet to your programs. So waking up from your emotions isn't denying you have them or seeing them as an inconvenience. Rather it is learning to navigate them in a way that no longer sends you back to sleep.

## Navigating Emotional Hijacks from Others

Most of us have a much easier time practicing awareness in our homes or during meditation, than we do in the real world. When you encounter other humans who are operating from their own triggers, it can often feel like an emotional hijack or an assault on your world. The real work is to be able to process how the hijack makes you feel, while simultaneously being able to see with clarity in that moment. You see that person as operating

from within their own emotional triggers, and you recognize the mirror of how you do the same at times. You don't tolerate aggression, anger or violence, but you learn to have the same awareness around the emotional triggers of others as you do around your own. Eventually, with practice, you'll be able to meet that person with compassion and love (while still maintaining clear boundaries and being firm with unacceptable behavior).

This is a practice for intimate or close relationships, and out in the world with strangers. For example, I had an experience while waiting for a friend at a bar in Pittsburgh, when two ladies and a gentleman came up and asked if they could sit next to me. Although I was saving a seat, I moved down one seat to make room for them. My friend showed up with an additional two friends in tow. We hung around, taking turns sitting and standing. When the two ladies and one gentleman looked like they were about to leave, I asked them if we could grab their seats. One of the women responded, "You can have our fu*king seats once we have left." I imagined the Joel of old, and how quickly I would have adapted to her mood, but I was able to wake up before I reacted. Instead of returning the insult, I smiled and said, "Thank you very much." A few minutes later they stood to leave and the lady said "There's your fu*king seat," and again I remained calm and said, "Thank y'all so much." The key is, I wasn't pushing down how I felt or being submissive to her abrupt response. I was choosing not to meet her where she was at, and in doing so, avoided a chain of chemical responses in myself and her that would only have led to more inflammation and pain for all involved.

In time, your relationships and interactions with others evolve because of your own personal evolution. You change the way you respond, and it cuts through a lot of the inflammatory responses that you have been used to experiencing in the past.

## SUMMING UP

The Artemes System supports emotional development on a twofold path. In one aspect, you develop peace, compassion, kindness, and love for other human beings so that you take action to contribute to our world in a way that makes a difference to others. In the other aspect, you develop these qualities within yourself for your own growth.

### We looked at:

- The Three Brains:
  - **Original brain** - Reptilian in nature. Regulates survival.

  - **Limbic brain** - Emotional generator. Responds reflexively. One of its key elements is the amygdala: the control center for the threat-response and threat interpretation system.

  - **Third brain** - The cerebral cortex, or the higher center of our brain. Reflective, contemplative, and methodical. One of the key elements is the prefrontal cortex.

- The relationship between the prefrontal cortex and the amygdala. How the former can be "trained" to calm the latter, and how much of the personal work carried out with emotions in the Artemes Training begins to create this effect.

- How developing the prefrontal cortex makes us more compassionate and empathetic as human beings, and how this supports our motivation to be part of the Artemes Training, so that we can create a fairer world for all.

- How, on our personal journey, Artemes does not reject emotions like some spiritual paths do. Instead, it supports you to navigate and integrate them.

- How navigating your own emotional experience involves recognizing that many emotions get triggered due to survival.

- How our life experiences—particularly the stressful or traumatic ones—become imprinted in our subconscious for a very specific reason. *Our subconscious mind is trying to protect us from experiencing something negative, and it creates a warning response, so that we don't repeat the same issues over and over again.*

- How unless we find a way to process the information that is held on a subconscious level relating to stressful or traumatic events that we experienced in the past, we can find ourselves reliving those events over and over again.

- How we learn to work with emotions, in Artemes, rather than reacting to them. We face our emotional hijacks and we develop ways to effectively process them so they are no longer running the show. This takes time and practice as the brain has been wired, through repetition, to react in certain ways.

- How we need to create strategies when we are not triggered that allow us to easily reconnect to the higher centers of our brain. This includes strategies for when others emotionally hijack us too.

Now that we have looked at how to respond to both psychological and emotional triggers, in the next chapter we will look at how the ultimate aim of Artemes is that you live a joyful life, contributing to others from a place of compassion. We'll explore some of the strategies—and pitfalls—of this aim in the next, and final, chapter.

# CHAPTER NINE
## AWAKENING TO THIS LIFE

> *Our species will either evolve to a more heart-centered consciousness, choosing a greater reverence for planet & people, or we will go extinct due to collective behavior too maladaptive for our survival. Each of us helps to choose which, through our own efforts & choices & love.*
> **Marianne Williamson on Twitter**

One of the most powerful gifts you can give yourself is to fully awaken to, and embrace, this life.

Much of the work that we have done so far has been focused on the parts of you that are still asleep. But one of the most fundamental tenets of the Artemes Training is to live a joyful, heart-centered, peaceful, and loving life.

Many of us have assumed that it's not possible, or even ethical, to do so in the current climate. There are many popular misconceptions and misunderstandings around our ability—or our right—to live in joy when at times it feels like the whole world is burning. In this chapter we'll be looking at why that choice is an essential one for the evolution of humanity.

## Choosing a Path of Joy

The core of spiritual teachings is to help each of us to either return to, or discover, the values of compassion, peace, and unconditional love. From there we can break down the prejudices, bigotries, misperceptions, and training that divide the whole world into "an 'us' that is good" and "a 'them' that we need to defeat."

Before we get into the how and the why, it's essential to highlight that when we choose a path of joy with Artemes, it does not mean we are ignoring the plight of others, glossing over issues, or bypassing that which needs to be dealt with in our collective experience of humanity. In fact, the opposite is true. As has been highlighted frequently throughout this book, the Artemes path is one where we choose to take a profound and unwavering responsibility for our own inner state and, simultaneously, commit to contributing to the world around us. So choosing, and then learning, to take joy as a path is not a selfish act that we carry out as a privilege in isolation from the rest of the world. Instead, we take this path ourselves so that we can ultimately help others forge it too.

Time and again we've highlighted that when you live from your highest state, free from doubt or fear, no matter what your circumstances, you are much more creative in your approach to finding solutions. Within this state, ideas generate from consciousness and not from protection or survival. When we cultivate our higher states, we generate more compassion for others, we feel love for all (rather than saying we love everyone while secretly feeling divided), we operate from our deepest desires to create change in the world, and we fearlessly move forward. This is the core of Artemes, and getting to this place is the central premise of the training.

## Creating an Authentic Path

In the book *My Stroke of Insight*, brain scientist Jill Bolte Taylor details how her experience changed when she suffered a severe stroke. She writes about how she sees reality after the loss of much of her left-brain faculties:

> *I morphed from feeling small and isolated to feeling enormous and expansive. I stopped thinking in language and shifted to taking new pictures of what was going on in the present moment. I was not capable of deliberating about past or future-related ideas because those cells were incapacitated. All I could perceive was right here, right now, and it was beautiful.*

> *My entire self-concept shifted as I no longer perceived myself as a single, a solid identity with boundaries that separated me from the entities around me. I understood that at the most elementary level, I am a fluid. Of course I am a fluid! Everything around us, about us, among us, within us, and between us is made up of*

*atoms and molecules vibrating in space. Although the ego center of our language center prefers defining ourselves as individual and solid, most of us are aware that we are made up of trillions of cells, gallons of water, and ultimately everything about us exists in a constant and dynamic state of activity. My left hemisphere had been trained to perceive myself as solid, separate from others. Now, released from that restrictive circuitry, my right hemisphere relished in its attachment to the eternal flow. I was no longer isolated and alone. My soul was as big as the universe and frolicked with glee in a boundless sea.[1]*

The challenge is that this place that Taylor described can't be forced. Many spiritual paths that have gone before have taught gratitude, peace, love, and forgiveness. *Followers on those paths have heard those words and tried to force themselves into those states, without actually feeling them.* This is a pointless pursuit. We end up with a conflict inside ourselves, because those states, and the values they represent, make sense to us, but we speak of them without experiencing them. And so, we end up with a spiritual language that is often hollow and unfelt. We hear someone else speaking it and it feels off. We don't trust them or we feel a jarring in ourselves when we hear their hollow words.

With Artemes, we aim to take a more authentic and practical path to reaching these states. If you think back to the model we presented in chapter 2, we highlighted the following path, which we have broken down further in this Artemes Training:

Awareness → Thoughts + Emotions → Awakening

So first, your process started with a ton of awareness, shining the light on all the areas of your life where you have been sleeping. Then we looked at simultaneously addressing your thoughts and emotions. This included developing the thoughts and emotions that allowed you to become more expansive, and working with the thoughts and emotions that created contraction in you. Because nothing is denied and everything is embraced in the Artemes Training, it is less likely that you will end up bypassing or rejecting the parts of yourself that are at odds with your highest qualities. An undeveloped or inauthentic "spiritual personality" usually emerges when these parts are denied or pushed away.

## The First Crack in Your World

My own awakening occurred over time, with small cracks in the shell of my world eventually leading to fissures that created the crumbling of the shell. The first crack came from a seemingly ordinary moment in New York City. I had just finished a conference in Connecticut and was preparing to travel to Queens to visit a friend, when a guy that I met at the conference offered me a ride. As we drove, he told me of his adventures in Thailand and his plans to retire there one day to dive and enjoy the simple life. As I listened to him, I heard myself saying, "Why are we waiting for retirement until we live?" We crossed the George Washington Bridge and he dropped me off at the 175th Street Station with a handshake and a goodbye. The conversation was such a simple one, but it had primed me in a way, and the subway ride south through Manhattan only intensified my thoughts on life. I asked myself, again, "What are you waiting for? What do you think is going to be available at retirement that isn't available now?" I felt a rush of adrenalin as I truly questioned my reality. "Why the fuck am I killing

myself in this moment for something so far off and so unknown?" By the time the train pulled into Penn Station, I was already feeling that the shell of my world was cracking. And that was just the beginning.

I share this story with you because the crack in my world wasn't, on its own, a remarkable moment in life. I hadn't run into a burning building to save a child, survived a disaster or been diagnosed with a life-threatening disease. I had, however, seen through the very trivial nature of the existence I had chosen. And once you have that moment, where you see through it all, you can never really look back.

## GIVE YOURSELF TIME:

If nothing has cracked in your world yet, make sure you are giving yourself time. Although in the US we have been frequently told the mantra, "Fake it till you make it," this is one area of your life where you want to make sure you aren't perceiving a crack in your world with your mind that you don't actually feel in your heart. If nothing has changed in your perception or your reality, keep practicing the exercises—particularly the ones that are designed to generate more consciousness and awareness—and allow the crack to come, rather than thinking it has to be something you achieve.

## Generating Joy

We've highlighted the concepts behind living a joyful life, and there are several practices and approaches that enable you to cultivate these states. Many of these states are generated from the relationship you develop with your nervous system.

Back in chapter 8 on emotions, we discussed how once survival mode has been activated, it keeps you locked in fear. This fear changes your perception of your reality as a whole, making you look through a narrow window to protect you from perceived threats. If you recall, much of the work that we need to do when we are in a perceived state of threat involves calming the amygdala and creating a connection with the prefrontal cortex (that higher center of the brain). When you are operating from the prefrontal cortex, you naturally experience a more expansive viewpoint, remaining connected to the higher centers of consciousness in your brain. Both our individual awakening and our contribution to transforming world challenges need to come from a place of thriving, rather than survival. This means that from a very practical standpoint, we need to be able to develop tools and practices that take us out of a sympathetic (fight or flight) nervous system state, and put us into a parasympathetic (rest and digest) nervous system state. From here, we can operate from higher levels of consciousness.

In chapter 7 we started to explore the space in between things. You may have noticed that if you have continued to practice these exercises, your nervous system instantly changes when you take your focus off objects and place it in the space in between those objects. The work that we will do in this section builds on that. We need to develop your relationship to stillness so that your nervous system gets an opportunity to reset.

This does not mean you reject movement altogether. Your most profound experiences of embracing this life will likely come when

you have developed a balance between movement and stillness. In an ideal scenario, the movement you create will challenge your muscles, fill your body with oxygen, get your heart pumping, take you out in nature, enable you to fully connect with the feeling of being alive. In contrast, your stillness will create a full reset of the nervous system, so that you develop practices that enable you to sit, or lie, in complete presence and stillness of body and mind.

## It's NOT an Attachment to Feeling Good

At the same time, we are <u>not</u> fostering an attachment to feeling good.

I experienced this attachment to feeling good when I ran the bar at Summit City with my then partner, which could best be referred to as a 10-year weekend!

At that time, amidst the cocktail of alcohol and endless partying, there was one belief that sat in the center of everything I held true: As human beings we are *supposed* to feel good.

This belief isn't just common to partying. It's behind much of what we do. The same driving force that had me downing shots night after night is probably showing up in some way within you too. When you think about it, a big part of what we eat, drink, buy or do centers around wanting to feel good, and a good chunk of our actions can be boiled down to one of two motivations: We are either chasing a feeling because we believe it will feel good or trying to rid ourselves of one that we don't want to feel anymore.

This shows up not only in our actions, but in our reactions. Have you ever noticed, for example, how disappointed you are when you don't feel good? Our tendency to feel like we are winning when we feel good, and losing when we don't, is a central part of our conditioning, particularly within a Westernized, capitalist society. This is mainly because it's easy to sell you a dream of feeling good, especially when you don't, and our whole society is set up for quick fixes and distractions to escape that feeling of dissatisfaction. Advertisers play into this constant desire to feel good too, either pushing your pain-points because they know you want to feel better, or showing you a fantasy of how much better you could feel in a future moment. And so you become trained to reach outside of yourself for a solution to that nagging feeling within you.

Most of us have been taught that joy is a feeling of euphoria. When we think joy is a feeling, we chase it like a drug. We arrange our external world—our relationships, our environment, our work—so that we can 'move closer to joy.' We lose our shit when those pieces don't behave as we hoped they would and we feel like we have moved further away from joy. When I talk about joy in the Artemes System, I'm not referring to that fleeting feeling that comes and goes. Instead, I'm talking about a way of showing up in the world that is *independent of how you feel.* This kind of joy might be accompanied by euphoria, excitement, and other emotions, but it's more *a slow, steady presence that sits at the center of everything you do.* It's a state that already exists within you, that you can nurture and support, rather than one that you need to fix, add to or control. You care for it, so that you create the context in which it can thrive, and you make your contribution to the world from that place.

So, we're working on the notion that you have more influence on your own inner climate than you might have previously thought, but this doesn't mean trying to constantly control your inner state or becoming obsessed with being happy. It doesn't mean placing your focus on creating a 'superior' version of yourself or becoming a superhuman. It does mean that you no longer have to feel that your inner climate is left to chance, and instead is deeply cared for.

> **EXERCISE:** Next time you have a 'difficult' emotion, notice that there is (1) the feeling itself, (2) the rejection of the feeling and (3) the story about how the feeling shouldn't be there.

When you carry out the exercise above you may notice, for example, that the cup of coffee you have, or piece of chocolate you eat, is an instant gratifier. This often takes place on such a subtle level that we don't think about it. Even when we know, deep down, that we are using stimulators to feel good throughout the day, many of the times we use them are automated responses to a subtle change inside us.

If you ever saw the film *The Matrix*, you might recall the scene where the lead character, Neo, learns to dodge bullets by seeing how they aren't real. When you first start carrying out this exercise, you might feel like Neo, except you are dodging the imaginary bullets from within. It's an opportunity to assess how many of your long-standing patterns might just be a knee-jerk reaction to a feeling that you have been trained to fix.

Waking up to the true nature of your conditioned responses around feeling good doesn't mean that you have to give up experiencing joy from outside sources. Many Eastern teachings have suggested that you have to choose between your inner world and your outer world, and this is where these kinds of teachings create a division within us. You don't have to choose between internally generated joy and the joy that comes from your external world. You can simultaneously engage in both, generating joy within and fully embracing life too. The difference is that when you are able to generate joy from within, it changes your relationship to the stimulators you use or the things that you accumulate in life, because you don't depend on them for your happiness; you don't need them to feel good. They become the object of a choice that you may or may not make, rather than being central to your happiness.

> **EXERCISE:** If you haven't previously considered how much attachment you have to feeling good, spend a couple of days looking at how you depend on instant gratifications. For most of us, treats, pick-me-ups, thrills, and rewards are woven into our day without a second thought. At the root of it, it's clear that there's a similar pattern in all of us. We notice that we don't feel good, we reject how we feel, and then we reach for something to change that.

There is an alternative to this familiar pattern, and it starts with a willingness to be deeply OK with however you feel. That doesn't mean you can't use a tool, a technique or a process to change your state, and in the Artemes Training, we've looked at hacking how you feel so that

you are able to shift yourself with tools and practices. However, when you start by being OK with whatever you feel, you approach your practices with a less desperate quality. You are curious about how you can create a change in yourself without needing to control the state you are in, or how you can take yourself beyond going for an instant gratification to fix how you feel.

## Becoming OK with However You Feel

In his book *Awareness*, which we mentioned earlier, Anthony De Mello shares one of his most memorable quotes: "Before enlightenment, I used to be depressed: after enlightenment, I continue to be depressed. But there's a difference: I don't identify with it anymore."[2] De Mello was a Jesuit priest who made waves in the '80s when he experienced enlightenment and continued to teach in the Catholic church, incorporating his enlightened perspective. The quote above describes the core of being OK with how you feel: Having a challenging emotion without identifying with it or becoming it. If you were raised with Western values, you were likely entrained to do the opposite. When we experience a difficult emotion, we are taught to say, "*I* am sad," "*I* am depressed," "*I* am down," so that we identify ourselves with the emotion. We also learn to believe that the emotion is a 'problem'. Rather, if there is a problem at all, it is in how we relate to our challenging feelings. We resist them. We push them away. This behavior might seem natural, but it is actually one that we've been taught.

In his quote, de Mello also highlights the misperception that 'enlightenment' or 'awakening' is going to bring one mood of joy, peace, and love all the time. This misperception is not present only for those on a spiritual path—we see it in all walks of life. We find ourselves fantasizing about a point in life where we will constantly feel good. We keep rearranging the furniture of our life in the hope that we will someday achieve this fantasy. We also continue to be disappointed if we don't. As the philosopher Alan Watts once said: "We don't blame the peaks for being high, or the valleys for being low." We accept the peaks and troughs in nature, but not in *our own* nature. Instead, we feel there is something wrong with us as we go up and down, and we learn to fix it with things that we buy or consume.

When we can get beyond our constant desire to feel good, there is a part of us that is free from suffering—a part of us that knows that pain is an inevitable part of our human experience, but suffering is often a choice. Suffering can be described as the story of the pain, the resistance to it, and the belief that it shouldn't be there. Beyond that there is that part of us that can feel the pain (whether physical or emotional) without getting lost in the narrative of it. When we know how to feel pain without suffering, we literally have the keys to the kingdom, because *nothing* can really touch us from there.

We can experience this freedom in a number of ways:

1. Whatever I think or feel, it can't touch my core
2. Whatever anyone thinks of me or says about me, it can't touch my core
3. Whatever happens to me, it can't touch my core.

Some people experience a greater freedom in one of these areas and not in the others. For example, after our work on the mind in

chapter 7, perhaps you've noticed that you derail yourself with certain thought patterns, but are untouched by the judgment of another. Much of the work we are doing in the Artemes Training is designed to develop a connection with the core of you that is already free—the part of you that exists in peace, love, and joy beyond the fluctuation of your thoughts and emotions, of the behaviors of others, the social climate, and the movement of the world around you. You might still get triggered by something in your external world, experience a low mood or get sick. You might still be heartbroken by a natural disaster or terrorist act. You might feel sadness and helplessness at some of the challenges that we are collectively facing right now. But despite the highs and the lows, you gradually find yourself experiencing the disruption, and the connection with your core, at the same time.

## Developing Your Purpose

The other major aspect of living a joyful life is developing a sense of purpose that makes you feel like you are deeply contributing to the challenges of these times.

Earlier we talked about roles. As far as your roles go, you need to be aware of anywhere that you overly identify with your achievements or goals. Artemes is not a goalless path. Your purpose is an essential part of who you are, here on this planet, and we need to look at ways of working towards, and deeply integrating, your purpose so that you have a sense of contribution and meaning to this world. Where it becomes a challenge is when your purpose is more important than being in the present moment. If you have already done something incredible with your life and you attach to who you were in the past, or if you think that a qualification or achievement is going to make you more than you are now, then achievement has taken over. The real art is to be engaged and excited in your goals without a) thinking they are going to give you more of yourself or b) hanging your identity on them. This is how we smash up the false pretext of the "American dream." We have been sold a version of reality where the more we achieve, the more we become. We have been taught to chase this dream above our sense of self: our identity is so closely tied with who we are becoming that we are barely able to see ourselves without it.

Personally, I got caught up in Apogee (my environmental firm) and Summit City (my bar) and this became my identity for a long time. I thought that I was winning in this thing called the American dream, but looking back, this was all a lie. All these so-called "achievements" were actually an excuse for me to build a false identity. Layer upon layer that covered the identity of my true self.

We have all likely made choices that have built up our roles, that keep us from our true selves. With the Artemes Training, we pull back those layers, one after another, until there is nothing left but your core.

## Noticing the Signs

You'll know you've begun to awaken when you no longer need to convince yourself that you are happy, or to achieve outside goals to feel good. True happiness is to enjoy the present, without anxious dependence upon the future—not to amuse ourselves with either hopes or fears, but to rest satisfied with what we have, which is sufficient.

When we are lost, we seek happiness in a new car, a vacation to the beach, running a marathon or getting a new job. All these things are from outside of us. We look for something to fill the hole in our soul. Yet if you are emanating happiness, none of these things have the same power over you. Drinking, partying, holidays. They take on a different quality. You don't do them because you are looking for something. When you do them from the space of joy, they are a bonus to an already content life. You already have it, so you are no longer searching for the outside to fulfill it. You truly enjoy the dance of life because you are not seeking to escape it.

To me, heaven is being in this moment, seeing myself in relation to the universe (and how insignificant and small I am) and considering space in this moment in time. Heaven is awareness. Waking up for me meant I existed in a space of open awareness where everything made sense. For you it might be something different. But you want to find that sweet spot where you are wide awake, able to catch yourself if you slip back into the dream, and simultaneously be guided by a passion to be here on this planet at this time, doing great things to contribute. If you're waiting on death to experience heaven, you are definitely missing the boat.

## SUMMING UP

One of the most powerful gifts you can give yourself is to fully awaken to, and embrace, this life. Much of the work that we have done so far has been focused on the parts of you that are still asleep. One of the most fundamental tenets of the Artemes Training is to live a joyful, heart-centered, peaceful, and loving life. This is not only essential for yourself, but also for the evolution of humanity.

### We looked at how:

- Choosing a path of joy does not mean ignoring the plight of others, glossing over issues, or bypassing social needs.

- The Artemes path is one where we choose to take a profound and unwavering responsibility for our own inner state and simultaneously, commit to contributing to the world around us.

- When we talk about joy, it is not something to be forced. It is also not an attachment to feeling good.

- Most of us have been taught that joy is a feeling of euphoria. When we think joy is a feeling, we chase it like a drug.

- In Artemes, when we refer to joy, we are not referring to that fleeting feeling that comes and goes. Instead, we're talking about a way of showing up in the world that is *independent of how you feel*. It's more *a slow, steady presence that sits at the center of everything you do.*

- Much of our society's advertising is focused on instant gratifiers that distract us from how we feel.

- When we can get beyond our constant desire to feel good, there is a part of us that is free from suffering. We can experience this freedom in a number of ways:

    o Whatever I think or feel, it can't touch my core

    o Whatever anyone thinks of me or says about me, it can't touch my core

    o Whatever happens to me, it can't touch my core.

The other major piece of living a joyful life is developing a sense of purpose that makes you feel like you are deeply contributing to the challenges of these current times.

# CONCLUSION

At this point in history, we each have much more power to effect change than we may have been led to believe. In this book I have shared how each of our individual decisions can contribute to being part of the solution, or create more of the same, and how we can come together to create a system that benefits the whole.

One of the most important understandings as you move forward in these times is that we have not only hope for the future, but also the power within us to create that change. Historian Howard Zinn reminds us:

> *To be hopeful in bad times is not just foolishly romantic. It is based on the fact that human history is a history not only of cruelty, but also of compassion, sacrifice, courage, kindness.*

*What we choose to emphasize in this complex history will determine our lives. If we see only the worst, it destroys our capacity to do something. If we remember those times and places—and there are so many—where people have behaved magnificently, this gives us the energy to act, and at least the possibility of sending this spinning top of a world in a different direction.*

*And if we do act, in however small a way, we don't have to wait for some grand utopian future. The future is an infinite succession of presents, and to live now as we think human beings should live, in defiance of all that is bad around us, is itself a marvelous victory.[1]*

This is the choice we must make in these times if we want to contribute to creating a different world order.

In this book we have shared not only a hope for a new socio-economic system that can disrupt the current economy, but a strategy to make it happen. We've highlighted that your own awareness and awakening is a crucial part of your motivation to be part of that change, and we've shared tools and strategies to support you on your way. It took 1,000 years for Buddhism to spread to Japan. It took 1,500 years for Christianity to expand from the Middle East to the Americas. Yet today an idea can cover the entire earth almost instantaneously. The power is in your hands to step into the Artemes System, and contribute to being part of that change.

# RESOURCES

For all the links to the articles
presented in this book visit:

**Artemes.global/book-resources**

Visit **artemes.global**
to join the revolution.

# ACKNOWLEDGMENTS

We all stand on the shoulders of those who came before us. The strong-shouldered beings I would like to thank include my mom (Alice) and dad (Everett). Daddy always joked that the Beverlys were bohemians, and then set off to prove the point. Mommy worked her ass off from the day she was born to the day she died. I am somehow a mix of those two.

Thanks to all my dear friends and personal gurus that I have had including Sharon, Rhonda, Adam, Daniel, Alec, Amelia, Mark, John, Bob, Quent, Dave, Todd, Kev, Anthony, Stephen, Carol, George, Mike, Beth, Rich, Dee, Becky, Dan, Mammad, and many others who I am missing here.

Thank you to Sasha, whose beautiful tutelage made writing this book possible. Also to Lois for your editing skills.

And thank you to my loving partner, Fern.

# ENDNOTES

## Chapter One

1. Aziz Ansari commented in his 2019 Netflix show *Right Now, minute 2.50*
2. Marianne Williamson in an interview with comedian and activist, Russell Brand, https://www.youtube.com/watch?v=8mP4As8FJAc, *minute 42.47*
3. https://www.foodbanknyc.org/research-reports/?gclid=EAIaIQobCh-MIv7qG1ePp5AIVAobICh38_wDUEAAYASAAEgI6kfD_BwE
4. https://www.frac.org/maps/acs-poverty/acs-poverty.html
5. https://www.equities.com/is-the-capitalist-system-really-broken
6. Therborn, Göran, *The Killing Fields of Inequality*, Polity, Cambridge, 2013, p 21
7. Ibid. p 170
8  Frankl, Viktor E., *Man's Search for Meaning*, Beacon Press, Boston, 2006

## Chapter Two

1  https://www.huffpost.com/entry/10-people-who-came-out-of_n_4086176

# Chapter Three

1   Sachs, Jeffrey D., *The End of Poverty: Economic Possibilities for Our Time*, Penguin, New York, 2015, p 315-317

2   Williamson, Marianne, *A Politics of Love: A Handbook for a New American Revolution*, Harper One, New York, 2019, p 8

3   Sachs, Jeffrey D., *The End of Poverty: Economic Possibilities for Our Time*, Penguin, New York, 2015, p 28

4   Ibid.

5   https://www.theguardian.com/global-development/2017/jan/16/worlds-eight-richest-people-have-same-wealth-as-poorest-50

6   http://piketty.pse.ens.fr/files/capital21c/en/Piketty2014FiguresTables.pdf

7   http://datatopics.worldbank.org/gmr/palma-index.html

8   https://www.technologyreview.com/s/610395/if-youre-so-smart-why-arent-you-rich-turns-out-its-just-chance/

9   https://www.worldvision.org/sponsorship-news-stories/global-poverty-facts

10  http://sewabharat.org/wp-content/uploads/2015/07/Report-on-Unconditional-Cash-Transfer-Pilot-Project-in-Madhya-Pradesh.pdf

11  https://doc-research.org/2018/03/will-universal-basic-income-change-lives/

12  https://economicprinciples.org/Why-and-How-Capitalism-Needs-To-Be-Reformed/

13  https://finance.yahoo.com/news/ray-dalio-worries-capitalism-could-205134758.html

14  https://www.theverge.com/interface/2019/10/23/20927076/marc-benioff-trailblazer-book-salesforce-ceo-capitalism

15  Williamson, Marianne, *A Politics of Love: A Handbook for a New American Revolution*, Harper One, New York, 2019, p 7-8

16  Leen Abdallah, "The Cost to End World Hunger," Borgen Project, February 15, 2015, https://borgenproject.org/the-cost-to-end-world-hunger/

17  https://www.forbes.com/billionaires/#66d81c54251c

18  "Hunger and Poverty Facts," Feeding America, accessed July 16, 2018, http://www.feedingamerica.org/hunger-in-america/hunger-and-poverty-facts.html.

19  Adam Tschorn, "Americans just spent $60.59 billion on pets. A by-the-numbers look at our obsession," Los Angeles Times, June 20, 2015, http://www.latimes.com/style/pets/la-hm-pets-index-20150620-story.html.

20  Debbie Phillips-Donaldson, "Global pet care sales pass $100 billion for first time," Pet Food Industry, February 7, 2017

21  https://www.mercurynews.com/2017/10/03/holiday-shopping-young-shoppers-are-willing-to-spend-on-gifts-for-pets/

22  Chloe Sorvino, "Why The $445 Billion Beauty Industry is a Gold Mine for Self-Made Women," Forbes, May 18, 2017 https://www.forbes.com/sites/chloesorvino/2017/05/18/self-made-women-wealth-beauty-gold-mine/#904fec32a3a5

23  "Global fashion industry statistics – International apparel," Fashion United, accessed July 16, 2018, https://fashionunited.com/global-fashion-industry-statistics.

24  Elizabeth Weise, "Cyber Monday: Biggest online shopping day in U.S. history pits Amazon vs. Walmart," USA Today, November 27, 2017

25  https://www.usatoday.com/story/money/2018/11/27/cyber-monday-sales-7-9-billion-top-record-online-sales-estimate/2123414002/

26  https://www.huffpost.com/entry/10-people-who-came-out-of_n_4086176

27  Vidal, Gore, *History of the National Security State*, The Real News Network, *2014,* p 70

28  https://www.sciencedirect.com/science/article/pii/S0006320718313636

## Chapter Four

1  Williamson, Marianne, *A Politics of Love: A Handbook for a New American Revolution,* Harper One, New York, 2019, p 49

2  https://www.vox.com/future-perfect/2019/1/22/18192774/oxfam-inequality-report-2019-davos-wealth

3  http://www.joseluisdiaz.org/wp-content/uploads/2011/04/Perception-Suffering_MenWomen_Mercadillo2011.pdf

## Chapter Five

1  https://www.bloomberg.com/news/articles/2017-11-29/bitcoin-ought-to-be-outlawed-nobel-prize-winner-stiglitz-says-jal10hxd

2  Yunus, Muhammad, *Building Social Business: The New Kind of Capitalism that Serves Humanity's Most Pressing Needs,* Public Affairs Books, New York, 2010, p 72-73

3  Milanovic, Branko, *Global Inequality: A New Approach for the Age of Globalization,* Belknap, Harvard, 2016, p 150

4  Giridharadas, Anand, *Winners Take All: The Elite Charade of Changing the World,* Vintage Books, Random House, 2019, p 43

5  https://www.investopedia.com/articles/forex/121815/bit-coins-price-history.asp

6  Bishop, Matthew and Green, Michael, *Philanthropic Capitalism, How the Rich Can Save the World,* 2008,

7  https://financesonline.com/top-10-most-expensive-air-jordan-sneak-ers-ever-sold-michael-jordans-flu-game-shoes-top-the-list/

8  https://financesonline.com/top-10-most-expensive-air-jordan-sneak-ers-ever-sold-michael-jordans-flu-game-shoes-top-the-list/

9  https://financesonline.com/top-10-most-expensive-air-jordan-sneak-ers-ever-sold-michael-jordans-flu-game-shoes-top-the-list/

10  Therborn, Göran, *The Killing Fields of Inequality,* Polity, Cambridge, 2013, p 58

11  https://www.investopedia.com/terms/p/prisoners-dilemma.asp, Sept 27, 2019

12  PDF of slides:  https://vitalik.ca/files/intro_cryptoeconomics.pdf

13  full breakdown of slides: https://www.youtube.com/watch?v=pKqdjaH1dRo

14  Yunus, Muhammad, *Building Social Business: The New Kind of Capitalism that Serves Humanity's Most Pressing Needs,* Public Affairs Books, New York, 2010, p 107

15  https://digiconomist.net/bitcoin-energy-consumption

## Chapter Six

1   Chalmers, David J., *The Conscious Mind: In Search of a Fundamental Theory*, Oxford University Press, New York, 1996

2   de Mello, Anthony, Awareness: *The Perils and Opportunities of Reality*, The Center for Spiritual Exchange, Image Books, Doubleday, p 3

3   Ibid. p 4

4   A 2010 *Psychological Science* study by MacLean et al. https://www.ncbi.nlm.nih.gov/pubmed/20483826

5   https://fightthenewdrug.org/by-the-numbers-see-how-many-people-are-watching-porn-today/

6   https://www.rescuingleftovercuisine.org

## Chapter Eight

1   Perlmutter, MD, David and Austin, *Brain Wash: Detox Your Mind for Clearer Thinking, Deeper Relationships, and Lasting Happiness*, p 27-33

2   Ibid. p 27

3   Ibid. p 28-31

4   Ibid. p 32

5   Ibid. p 33

6   https://physicalliving.com/how-much-should-i-be-able-to-deadlift/

## Chapter Nine

1   Bolte Taylor, Jill, *My Stroke of Insight: A Brain Scientist's Personal Journey*, Penguin, New York, 2009, p 71

2   de Mello, Anthony, *Awareness: The Perils and Opportunities of Reality*, The Center for Spiritual Exchange, Image Books, Doubleday, p 61

## Conclusion

1   Howard Zinn, "The Optimism of Uncertainty," *The Nation*, September 2, 2004, https://www.thenation.com/article/optimism-uncertainty/

# ABOUT THE AUTHOR

Joel Beverly is an edgewalker who has united the worlds of spirituality and economics, combining them into a brand new system that he has called Artemes. He is not simply a visionary with a dream. He is a leader who has created a path for redefining the economic structures of the world.

Beverly grew up in one of the poorest areas of the US, and he lived through extreme socio-economic challenges firsthand. After paving a different path for himself, he became a serial entrepreneur, creating many different companies, and hundreds of jobs in his community.

The Artemes book was launched on Nov 16th, 2020, and within less than 24 hours, become a #1 global bestseller in the self-help sector and a #3 global bestseller in the business sector.

## Amazon Best Sellers
Our most popular products based on sales. Updated hourly.

**Best Sellers in Spiritual Self-Help**

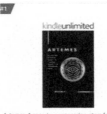

Artemes: A conscious economic system for...
› Joel Beverly

365 Quotes to Live Your Life By: Powerful,...
› I. C. Robledo

The Secret to Everything: How to Live More and...
› Neel Burton

## Amazon Best Sellers
Our most popular products based on sales. Updated hourly.

**Best Sellers in Business & Investing**

Start Finishing: How to Go from Idea to Done
› Charlie Gilkey

Online Men's Groups Success: A Step-by-Step...
Kenny Mammarella-D'Cruz FRSA

Artemes: A conscious economic system for...
› Joel Beverly

Join the movement:
https://Artemes.global